The **R***isk* **T***akers*

C**HRISTINE** L**EONARD**

Scripture Union

By the same author:
Children on the Edge
Hidden in the Mist – Leopard

© Christine Leonard 1997
First published 1997
Reprinted 1998

Scripture Union, 207–209 Queensway, Bletchley,
Milton Keynes, MK2 2EB, England.

ISBN 1 85999 168 8

British Library Cataloguing-in-Publication Data.
A catalogue record of this book is available from the British
Library.

Printed and bound in Great Britain by Cox & Wyman Ltd,
Reading.

Contents

Thank you

To all the people who have helped me find out information for this book, and special thanks to those whose stories are told here. I learnt a great deal through meeting many of them. I realised that they feel frightened or weak at times and don't always have a 'hot line' to God, yet they still keep giving their lives for him. Each is very different, but each has shown me how much God can do through a person, if only we will let him!

How to help or find out more

You can write to an address given at the end of most chapters. Don't forget to include a stamped, self-addressed envelope for addresses in this country or International Reply Coupons for abroad. You can buy these at a Post Office.

Steve Chalke
– working with poor people in London and across the world

You might have seen Steve on television, or heard him on the radio, but an awful lot happened before that! Here's his story.

Oasis – Going for a Dream

It all began when I was fourteen and fell in love with Mary Hooper. Because she went to London's South Norwood youth club I started going along too, but she was a whole year older than me and would only look at guys aged sixteen and over!

I kept wondering, how could I get to know the girl of my dreams with all this unfair competition around? Then I found out something very strange. Mary went to church on Sundays! I'd done the same when I was a kid but I'd given it up years ago. Still, Mary might notice me there! The first Sunday, I couldn't believe it. Those enormous pews – a great place to huddle up to your girlfriend! All through the service I edged closer to Mary.

The weeks passed. Slowly it became clear that Mary would never go out with me. A few of the things I'd heard in church must have sunk into my brain, though. Wandering home one Sunday night, I began thinking. If all that was true – if God really loved people so much that he sent Jesus to give his life for them – well the least I could do in return was to give my own life to God. On the other hand, if it wasn't true – then why keep going to church, even if Mary Hooper was the best looking girl in the world?

Right there and then in Dixon Road, South Norwood, I decided to become a Christian. Somehow I knew that I would spend my life telling others about Jesus. I had a very strong feeling that God was asking me to work among the poor – in particular to set up a hostel, a hospital and a school for them. It came to me as clear as that – talk about a big dream!

I started by going up to London on Friday nights with a few friends, a flask of soup and some sandwiches. We'd spend the night sharing food and getting to know the homeless people who sheltered under the arches near Charing Cross Station.

Today, London is a far more violent place and fourteen year olds would not be wise to do this kind of thing. But twenty-five years ago I could not get over how young most of the homeless people were. I'd expected to find men who had fought in the Second, or even First World War – but these were teenagers who had been thrown out of their homes. Some had run away because their families had split up, others because their parents beat them, or because they hated council care.

One Friday I asked, 'Where's Graham?' I'd got to know this teenager quite well.

'Found dead on a park bench last Tuesday,' someone replied.

I never found out exactly why Graham died. It could have been from a drug overdose, from the cold, or from an illness like pneumonia. Whatever the reason, Graham was there one week and gone forever the next. I never forgot it. Over the months others died and I became even more sure that I had to spend my life helping people like them.

After school I trained as a Baptist minister, then started work in a Kent church. From the beginning I helped the church's young people get involved – not just in talking and singing about God and the things they believed, but in doing things. They would pray and work and plan together and maybe get permission to use an empty shop to put on a concert or play. It worked really well. Soon I was talking to young people all over the country and helping them get projects started.

By this time I had married ... not Mary Hooper, but the true love of my life, Cornelia! Both of us felt that it was time to open the hostel I had dreamt about all those years before. We found a building in Peckham and asked businessmen, bankers and charities for money so we could start the project.

No one gave anything. Then a lawyer friend of mine called Will Mattheson came round for lunch. He said, 'You need to make the hostel project into a charity – that makes it much easier for these people to give!'

'Right!' I said, my mouth full of fish and chips. 'How do we do that?'

'Well, first you need a name!'

'How about Oasis?' suggested Cornelia. 'It'd be like a place in the desert where people come for food and water and shelter!'

'Oasis Hostel?' It didn't sound that wonderful to me, but it was a name!

Will helped us set up the Oasis Trust, which raised the money. However, when the first hostel opened in Peckham in 1985, no one wanted to live in a place called Oasis. They called it Number 3, because that was its street number. People who had slept in shop doorways now had a home, with an address which sounded just like anyone else's.

In the end, the Oasis Trust became the name, not of the hostel, but of the work of the team of young people who helped us. It grew and grew until today, at any one time, over 200 work as volunteers for Oasis, praying and going out onto the streets to care for homeless people. Whenever a new hostel is opened, church youth groups arrive to strip the wallpaper, to paint and clean the house, to do the garden and to raise money too.

Oasis now runs two hostels in London, so the first thing God said to me came true. Part Two was to start a hospital. Well, now we have Lizzie's – the Elizabeth Baxter Health Care Centre, opposite the Imperial War Museum. Homeless people made 20,000 visits to Lizzie's in its first two and a half years for medical care or a shower. Oasis uses its own double-decker bus to find them on the streets and offer care, counselling, food and clothes.

The third thing God told me to do was to set up a school. Right now Oasis is planning one for Inner London children who have been permanently excluded from their own schools. These children can be as young as six or seven. Many are born into families which do not care for them or teach them about right and wrong. I want the Oasis school to give these children love and a new start.

Things started happening in other countries too, after I visited India in 1988 ...

A Cracker of an Idea

Once the Oasis projects were going well in London, I spent more time travelling around Britain, telling young people about Jesus. Then, in 1988, I was invited to India, mainly to talk to youth leaders about working with young people.

I knew about India of course, from things I had seen in newspapers and magazines or on the television – but photographs don't smell or spit or sweat, and if the television made too much noise I could always turn it down! Nothing had prepared me for India's largest city: Bombay. Its pavements were jammed solid with people who lived there because they had nowhere else to go. They had no running water for drinking or washing. Their bed was the pavement and their toilet the gutter. Whether young or old, people knew that things would never get better for them.

The next step up was living in a slum. Bombay has the largest one in the world, with over a million people. It's not good news. Half the babies born there die before their first birthday. I could not get over the heat, the smell, the filth, the numbers – but Falkland Road made me feel far worse. There around 60,000 prostitutes offer sex in exchange for money. Many are young girls, whose parents force them to earn cash this way. Lots become pregnant. Their babies may be left naked in the gutter or in a rubbish bin. Others survive, living on the streets with no one to look after them – thin, hungry, without enough to drink.

I felt terrible because I had so much – almost anyone in Britain did, compared with millions of Indians. Flying home on the plane, I knew I had to do something about the desperately poor people I had seen, but what? I started thinking about the way thousands of Christian young people had worked with Oasis. They would be only too willing to help, if someone gave them the chance!

'OK, you do it!' I told Christian youth groups all over Britain. 'We'll give you more information but basically you find an empty shop and get permission to use it for a month around Christmas time. Clean it, stick up some tinsel, borrow some microwaves – and then open as a restaurant.'

We called the project Christmas Cracker and that year each restaurant had a slogan – '*Eat Less – Pay More*'. They served the kind of simple meals which people eat in poor countries, but customers paid British restaurant prices. Young people prepared the food and waited at tables for free – and the profits helped start Oasis' new work in Bombay.

The idea really caught on. Many customers said they ate far too much at Christmas – and hated the way it had become such a greedy time. They saw Cracker as a great opportunity to give, instead of getting. Even more important than raising money, though, was the way young people got involved.

If being a Christian is about going to church on Sunday and reading your Bible and saying your prayers, to be honest most people find it all pretty boring after a while. Even with the liveliest Bible notes in the world and the most exciting worship and the best preacher, it's still more or less the same every week. But when you start doing things your faith comes to life – because suddenly you have something to pray about. You are desperate for an empty shop and cheap bread and for the entire team not to catch the 'flu that's going round! You slave away and pray like mad – and when it all actually works, it's brilliant. You'll thank and praise God – no trouble!

Soon some of the young people were doing even more important things. For example, John worked hard as a cook when his church youth club ran a Cracker restaurant that first year. After the group watched a video about Oasis' work in India, John decided to join a team which I was taking there. He enjoyed the three week trip so much that he longed to go again, but the next one was going to last three months. John talked his boss into giving him enough leave from his work.

Soon afterwards, Oasis needed someone who would look after new teams of young people who were coming to work in India for six months at a time. John took the job – and fell in love with an Indian girl called Charmaine. They married early in 1995 and now, after a year at Bible college, they want to spend the rest of their lives working among poor people in the slums of Bombay. And it all started with a bit of cooking!

Ruth trained in fashion design after she left school, and she too helped her church youth group with a Cracker project. Later she joined one of the teams John organised, working in Bombay's slums for six months. When I visited the team I started thinking of ways they could help the prostitutes and their children. Many women only became prostitutes to earn money so their children could go to school, which might lead to a better life for them. I wondered if we could teach these women other skills, so I talked to Ruth about setting up a tailoring business. If Oasis could teach them to sew and produce high quality clothes to sell back

11

in Britain, the women would earn good wages and the project would pay for itself.

Ruth stayed on in Bombay after her team's six months finished. She used her design skills to help set up the business, which they called Jacob's Well. One young British girl ended up changing the lives of hundreds of people. The BBC came and made a short film about it.

From 1989 – 1995 Cracker raised nearly £4 million through unusual ideas like its restaurants, newspapers, radio stations and Really Useful Present Shops – but the most important thing we do is to show people that their lives can make a difference. Young people don't want to stick forever on church pews praying, 'God bless the poor' when they could be out there doing something to help! It's not easy to work with homeless people in either London or Bombay – especially when they're sick all over the place, or if they smell. At times like that you know you need God's help to love them, so you pray. When you see that your faith works it's so exciting and you long to do more!

Oasis has helped set up many hostels, hospitals and schools in India and now we work in other poor countries, such as Tanzania and Brazil too. Christmas Cracker projects have been taken up by television or radio stations such as GMTV and Radio One. It's amazing to see God at work!

You can find out more about the work of Oasis Trust and the Christmas Cracker project by writing to: Oasis Trust, 87 Blackfriars Road, London, SE1 8HA.

Jasia Gazda, Poland

Does anyone want me?

Could I be adopted and not know it all this time? Jasia's thoughts whirled.

A woman had let the word slip out and now she looked ashamed suddenly, as though she had told a terrible secret. Jasia worried all the more. Could it be possible that Mamuska and Tatusiek were not her real mum and dad? In her head she could hear kids at school taunting unpopular children, calling them '*za swe*', which was a nasty way of saying 'adopted' in their Polish language. They meant, 'Your own parents gave you away, so why would anyone else want you?'

However much Mamuska and Tatusiek tried to comfort eleven year old Jasia, she pushed them to one side. When they told her that her real mother lived in the same Polish village, she covered her ears.

Gently, Tatusiek tried to tell her how it was she came to be their adopted daughter. 'You see, eleven years ago Mamuska learnt that she could not have children. You know how we love little ones, Jasia, and we were heartbroken. I had to go to work, but Mamuska prayed the same prayer as

13

Hannah in the Bible. Do you remember that story, Jasia? Hannah couldn't have children either and she said to God that, if he should give her one, the child would belong to him.' After Mamuska had asked God for a child, she took a walk, and saw Mila, pushing a pram.

'What's the matter, Mila?' Mamuska asked, for the woman was crying.

'I'm ill. I have to stay in hospital for a long time – and I may die. There's no one to look after my baby. I have to take her to the orphanage.'

Mamuska's heart started beating very fast. She told Mila about her prayer and then, very shyly, asked, 'I suppose you wouldn't let me look after the baby for you, Mila?'

'Mila stopped crying and stared at me,' Mamuska told Jasia. 'Then she smiled and said she knew that Tatusiek and I were the best people in the world to love and care for her baby. She said that now she could go to hospital without worrying so much about you. We signed some papers – and that's how you became our little girl.'

Jasia looked away.

'We adopted you, Jasia. We chose you. That makes you extra special to us!' Tatusiek squeezed her arm gently.

'And God chose you for us as well. It was like a miracle that day!' Mamuska was beaming her lovely smile, but Jasia would not look at her. She ran into her room and slammed the door. If they've not told me the truth all these years, why should I ever trust them again, she thought? I'm *za swe*. Even my own mother didn't want me. I'm second rate; everyone knows it. Well, I'll show them!

Over the next few years, as Jasia studied at

14

school and then at college, she turned her back on everything her parents believed in. They felt that the Communist rulers of Poland were doing the country no good – so Jasia worked hard at becoming everyone's favourite in the Communist youth groups and recited poems at rallies, to loud applause. Then she gained a place at a top college. Only the brightest students and the best Communists went there. She lived in the college, away from Tatusiek and Mamuska at last. Everything seemed to go well until she failed a science test. That meant losing a scholarship which she had wanted badly.

I can trust no one but myself and now I've let myself down, she thought. In despair, she tried to take her own life, but was rushed to hospital. Afterwards she talked with one of the few people she did admire. Jozef Prower was an old music professor at her college, and everyone who heard him teach or play the violin agreed that they had never heard anything so inspiring.

Jozef seemed so utterly happy within himself that Jasia could hardly believe it when he told her he too had once tried to commit suicide. 'I want you to read this book,' he said, handing it to her.

It had five pages, each of them a different colour, but Jasia could find no words or pictures at all. 'How's this going to help me?' she asked.

'Which page reminds you of your life right now?'

'That's easy – the black one!'

'And you know what makes our lives black, Jasia? Sin, selfishness and wrong things. But – the next page is golden, like sunshine, like the light of God.'

Jasia screwed up her eyes. 'God wouldn't want me spoiling his dazzling brightness with my dark thoughts!'

'Of course not – but he does long to know you, Jasia. That's why he sent his son, Jesus.' Jozef turned to the next page, which was bright red. 'Jesus had done no wrong. When he bled and died on the cross, it was to take the punishment which you and I deserve.'

Jozef turned the page, 'Now God can say to anyone who asks him for forgiveness, "Jesus paid the price, so that you can come and live in the sunshine of my love. I don't see the badness in you any more. I see you the same way I see Jesus – as bright light without any shadows in it."' Sure enough the last page was brilliant white.

'And the green page?'

'That's to remind you of trees and plants and everything that grows. If you follow Jesus, you will blossom, just as they do!'

Jasia found the message of the wordless book a bit much. Making an excuse, she walked off, miserable as ever.

A few weeks later she gave in. 'OK God, I've fought you long enough. I'm sorry. I don't want to live in this dark mess any more. Will you help me?'

At once she felt clean and new inside. Best of all, she knew that God had become her father. Being adopted into his family felt so good, as though she had come home. Tatusiek, Mamuska, Jozef and all the others who really cared about her were delighted. But, in the midst of her happiness, Jasia felt something very strongly. So many Polish children were in Communist youth organisations which taught them not to believe in God. They were lost in the dark, just as she had been. That same night she promised God to spend her life telling them how to become his children.

Years later, when she was busy doing just that, she heard a man speak at a Christian meeting, and he could have been talking about her. 'It's sad, but many people think that others don't want them,' Bruce explained. 'To protect themselves, they build walls in their hearts. Walls stop others getting too close, but they also shut people inside a prison where they feel second rate and sorry for themselves. Some become bitter or jealous of other people; others try to draw attention to themselves.'

Jasia could recognise all of those things in her own life. Even now she was grown up and knew Jesus well, she could see how some of the 'walls' which she had built still affected the way she thought about herself and treated others.

Bruce talked with her and they prayed together. Finally he said, 'Jasia, do you think you could forgive your real mother now?' Mila had died and Jasia had never got to know her real mother. Even though her mind understood that Mila had acted for the best, still Jasia felt hurt. Her own mother had given her away! She had to ask Jesus for help before she could say, 'Mila ... Mum, I forgive you.'

It was as though all the walls Jasia had built came tumbling down. Now she knew she wasn't second rate. The hurt which she had kept hidden for so long disappeared from her heart for ever.

Telling the Children

Soon after she became a Christian, Jasia left college and started teaching. The children loved her. What other class in this Communist school kept goldfish? They had a great time collecting moss and carving wooden figures to make a history corner, too!

At first the Headmistress praised Jasia for her wonderful new methods of teaching, until she found out that some of the lessons were about Jesus. Even worse, Jasia had recently refused to join the Communist party, because Communists do not believe in God. The Headmistress stormed into the classroom and swept the history corner into the rubbish bin. 'You children will catch germs from this dirty mess,' she shouted, '... and from these!' She flushed the goldfish down the toilet. Later Jasia found her beating one of the children.

How am I to do what God wants, she thought afterwards? I'm only trying to help the children to find something good, yet ugly things happen to them because of it! She told the whole story to her wise old friend, Jozef Prower. 'And even when the Communists do nothing to stop me, I'm not making Jesus real to the children!' she complained.

'Why not?' Jozef asked.

'Well, I love the children and they love me. I tell them stories about Jesus, and I'm not boasting, Jozef, but I'm good at it. They really listen and ask loads of questions. They're learning all about Jesus, just as they learn about kings and queens in history, but Jesus is different. They need to know him! How else can they hope to follow his teachings?'

Jozef smiled. 'Well ... I think you need two things, Jasia. One is prayer for protection. Sadly, it's dangerous to stand up for Jesus in our country at the moment. The second thing is training. I know just the thing: an Irishman called Sam is visiting me soon, and his organisation could help you learn how to introduce children to Jesus right across Poland!'

Before long Jasia went to hear Sam give a talk.

'I see lots of Sunday Schools that keep the children quiet and tell them nice stories about Jesus,' he said, 'but if they never meet him for themselves, what's the point?'

That's exactly what we were saying, Jasia whispered to Jozef. She listened carefully as Sam advised them to teach a group of children about Jesus in two ways. Suppose the point of the story was that Jesus wants us to be kind to people. The teacher should always make sure that those who do not know Jesus realise they need him to help them do this, and show them how to make him boss of their lives. For those who already knew Jesus, the story should teach them more about him, how to love him and do what he wants.

Jasia found Sam's talk so helpful that she longed to go on his organisation's three month training course in Switzerland. But that's impossible, she thought! No one left Poland without special permission and the Communist authorities were never going to let her go on a Christian course, were they? Also, the course was in English.

Jozef smiled, 'There's an old Polish saying, Jasia, "When you can't get in through the door, use the window!" God does some amazing things when we pray. Even when the "window" is barred, I've known him help people in through the "chimney"!'

Jozef knew a Christian lady in England. 'She's old and frail, so she needs some help in the house. I'm sure she'd teach you English in return,' he said.

Eventually Jasia won permission to go to England as au pair to this lady. She did not mention that on her way back to Poland she would stop off in Switzerland for Sam's course. Something else nearly kept her in England. An attractive British man fell in love and asked her to marry him. Jasia thought she loved him too, and life was so much easier in his country! She longed to be with him. But what would happen to all those children in Poland? She knew that they needed her, but found it very hard to say goodbye to Alistair!

After taking Sam's course in Switzerland, Jasia felt ready to tell millions of Polish children about Jesus. She could hardly wait! But the Communists were watching her. A man hung around outside her house and followed wherever she went. Jasia realised that she had to work carefully, so as not to put herself or the children in too much danger. She managed to lead some children's meetings and camps. After one meeting the church asked if she would come and work with children in her town.

'You know, they are calling you Mamuska (Mum) already!' one old lady at the church told her. 'Me too! I've been going to church for eighty years, but today you've helped me meet Jesus myself, for the first time ever!'

Jasia decided to move to the church. The Communists did what they could to stop her work, but she helped many children in that town to grow in their faith. By herself, Jasia could only help add a small number of children into God's family, but if these found others to join them, and those found more again, the numbers multiplied.

Although Jasia has never married or had any children of her own, today thousands of little ones all over Poland call her 'Mamuska', because she helped them get adopted into God's family. There are different rulers in Poland now and it is easier for Jasia to teach children about Jesus. The work grows and grows.

Joseph Kobo, Transkei, South Africa

Prisoner

Time – that was all he had now – except for a few thin clothes which did not keep out the cold. They had reopened Kieskamahoek jail especially for Joseph. To be the only prisoner in the whole, crazy mountain-top fortress was a strange honour – one he could have done without. No human voice had spoken to him for ... he tried not to think about how the years were passing.

Time had become his enemy. He had far too much of it. He could sleep, on and off, for a few hours. He could try to keep himself fit – and warm – by running on the spot, or by throwing punches at his pillow. Otherwise he was free only to think. Joseph thought a great deal during the three years he was in that prison cell.

He thought back over his childhood – growing up a herdsman's son in a Transkei village. Against all the odds he managed to get a good education – he'd shown them, all right!

Then that funny business after the big rally. He could hardly believe it now, but he'd got religion! He'd even trained, and worked, as a church pastor – gone all out for it too, until 'apartheid' came between black and white people, even in the church. To think that four million white people could herd sixteen million blacks into a few poor areas of the country they called 'homelands'. 'Apartheid' meant keeping the blacks separate. The government passed laws which meant Joseph's people could be flung into prison simply for going to certain places, in a country which had once been theirs.

Joseph had thought the churches would stand up for black people, but most of them didn't. He'd had no time for God since then. He left the church and later joined Umkhonto, the military wing of the African National Congress, who were fighting for the black people. They trained him as a guerilla and he started gun-running for them – smuggling supplies of weapons over the border from neighbouring countries. It was dangerous work, but he was good at it – bringing large loads mainly of AK47 assault carbines with their twenty-four round magazines. Sometimes he used a vehicle; he was known as one of the best drivers around and could handle anything. At other times he had waded crocodile-infested rivers carrying guns under the very eyes of the South African forces.

He had spent time in prison before – 1000 days in 1968-70 on the notorious Robben Island, joining his father's brother, Nelson Mandela, who had already spent six years there. In two other South African prisons he had been beaten and tortured, but had never known anything as bad as this ... this nothingness, this silence.

On Robben Island he mixed with the other prisoners and used his cell as a kind of office – arranging things for Umkhonto, which was probably why they had stopped him talking to anyone now! Later he had become a logistics officer – working out all the practical details of supplying the Umkhonto guerilla groups scattered across Southern Africa. Later still he was made an acting commander. Those were exciting days, living by the gun, danger round every corner, working out how to outwit the South African forces and intelligence organisations. He'd been tough and good at his job, respected by the men below and above him in the ANC.

But that was then. Now, in 1983, he was stuck in this freezing prison, high in the Drakensburg mountains of South Africa – and was starting to fear he would never get out, or speak to another human being again.

And then, one morning, one of the guards did speak, telling Joseph quite casually that his wife had died some months previously.

No, Joseph thought! Not Angelinah!

The rest of that day passed in a grief-filled daze. In the evening, Joseph heard another voice. It said, 'Why are you here?'

He understood the words – no trouble! But they didn't seem to be in any language he knew – not English or Afrikaans, not Russian or Xhosa. Joseph looked at the door – no guards around. The voice repeated the same words. But who was speaking?

Eventually Joseph tried answering. 'I'm here because I fought for the rights of my people.'

'Did I ask you to do it in that way, Joseph?'

Whose voice was that? Were the guards playing a trick on him? The more he thought about it the more impossible that seemed. The voice kept repeating the same questions. It couldn't be ... well,

God, could it? No, of course not.

Every day for three months Joseph heard the same voice asking the same questions. Finally he broke down, crying and sobbing. After some time he whispered, 'All right, God, if you really want me again, I'm here. I'll do whatever you say.'

After that, for the first time in many years, he felt a sense of peace. He slept for hours.

Within a few days, the guards began talking to him, and not long after that – out of the blue – the authorities decided to release him from prison. God can do things I never could, he thought. Now he was out he'd fight all right, but not with guns. He'd join a church and make a revolution for Jesus, a revolution which would change the hearts and minds of people in his country. But it was not going to be as easy as he'd imagined!

Revival

Joseph knew God wanted him when he became a Christian, but no one else seemed to. He'd been three years in prison – three years of speaking to no one – except for the last few weeks. Then he returned to his home village in the Transkei, brimming over with excitement. His rediscovered faith in God had given him a brand new start. But even his mother could not believe that he really had changed.

'No, son. I know you, you'll only cause trouble! Best leave now,' she said.

He travelled around. At every church he saw people exchanging looks, as if to say, 'This guy's dangerous.' He could understand it in a way. They all knew he had spent the past twenty years either in prison or as a terrorist in the ANC's military wing. Most wouldn't believe he had changed. They thought that he wanted to join their church only to stir up trouble, or to betray them in some way. And even if they accepted what he said, wouldn't the authorities be snooping around all the time, suspicious of everyone in the church which he had joined?

Joseph became more and more frustrated. He was as single-minded about serving God now as he had been fighting for the ANC – and he wanted to do something useful.

He talked to an old, retired bishop. 'What are you worried about, Joseph?' he said. 'God's with you, isn't he?'

'Sure, but ...'

'Well then, get out there and tell people about him. Start in the roughest place you can think of.'

The roughest place Joseph knew was a township outside the port of East London in South Africa. Few people there recognised him and he began by helping some of the local churches. He was good at getting alongside hard men: dockers, sailors, fighters, convicts. He'd been the toughest of the tough, a Communist-trained gun-runner. Now he told these men about Jesus. He was also good at organising things and training people, having been responsible for such matters with the terrorists. And he knew his Bible from his days as a pastor.

Very quickly the church authorities saw his worth. He was ordained as a pastor again, then made a bishop. One day, into his city office came three old men from the Transkei, where he had grown up. They looked much as Joseph's father used to, with blankets slung over their shoulders, and were carrying sticks for herding cattle.

'We want you to come to Lujizweni, to be our pastor,' they said.

Lujizweni? Joseph had to think hard. Wasn't that the place where he had first led a church, many years ago? It was a tiny village, miles from anywhere, its people the poorest of the poor. Didn't these country folk know he was a bishop now, doing all kinds of important things? He couldn't work there!

'Mrs Sicwetch has asked for you to come,' was all they said in explanation. Yes, Joseph remembered her, a woman of great faith, an outstanding Christian. He explained politely that he had too many things to do in East London. The men set off on the long journey home, adding only that Mrs Sicwetch and the Lujizweni church had been praying for Joseph since 1963. Joseph realised with a jolt that was the year he had turned his back on God. But he was too busy to think about the men's words for long.

The men kept returning. The third time Joseph decided that he would only get rid of them by paying the place a visit. By that time he had done some research. Lujizweni was in disgrace with the church authorities – because they prayed too much. 'They fast as well,' he was told. 'They go without food for days on end – very extreme. And your Mrs Sicwetch is the ring-leader.'

The church authorities had asked Lujizweni to behave more normally, but they would not listen, so their pastor and their church building were taken away from them. When Joseph visited the village in 1985 they were meeting in a round mud hut with a straw roof – someone's home. They haven't a clue, Joseph thought smugly.

Then they started the meeting. Joseph had never heard prayer like it. They prayed for South Africa, prayer as fierce as any fighting in a battle, only no one got hurt. They prayed for peace and for justice, for love to replace hatred, and Joseph knew that God was listening. No wonder things were beginning to change in his country. He felt very small when he recalled that these amazing people had been praying for him, Joseph Kobo, for 23 years!

Then a few got up and said what God had done for them – how he had turned their lives round and healed them. Incredible miracles had happened in that little, out-of-the-way place. This was for real, Joseph realised. It was what he had been looking for all those years – only he went about it in the wrong way. He had wanted to see an end to the terrible system of apartheid, where black people were kept separate from white and given the rough end of everything. He'd thought God and the church were doing nothing about it. He should have known that God hated injustice – but set about changing things through a revolution of love, not hate. God's warriors used prayer and divine power, not guns.

These Lujizweni prayer warriors had hold of something and it needed to break out – to spread right across the Transkei and beyond. Suddenly Joseph saw why Mrs Sicwetch had sent for him. He could help those things to happen.

When Joseph moved to the village he saw some of the miracles for himself. When they asked him to pray for a woman who had bled to death he was scared. She felt cold and stiff because she had been dead for hours. He dared not look at her as he prayed – and then suddenly she was standing up – not only alive, but well! Good news like that attracts more attention than an explosion – touching the lives of many more people than any bomb or hand-grenade could.

All Joseph's talents for organising and training people were needed as the church in Lujizweni spread the good news about Jesus around the area. Twenty churches like it had sprung up around the Transkei by 1987, and two years later had spread into other parts of South Africa. By 1993, over 100 churches like Lujizweni were growing right across the country, as more and more people heard the good news about Jesus and plugged into a powerful faith in him.

They kept praying for South Africa too. Everyone expected terrible bloodshed when the strict laws of apartheid were stopped, and the ANC finally took over government. But the new President, Nelson Mandela, talked of forgiveness. For twenty-six years Mandela had been a prisoner, most of the time on the notorious Robben Island, where his nephew, Joseph Kobo, had also been held for a while. But on his release Nelson Mandela urged everyone to forget the past, and to work together for a new future for the country, where all people would benefit.

Joseph has no inside knowledge about what went on in Nelson Mandela's heart or in the minds of the white rulers of South Africa. He only knows how God changed the way he himself thought and acted. He has seen how prayer changed things for hundreds and thousands of others. As revival sweeps across the land, they have woken up to a new faith, a new start and a new life following Jesus.

David Powe, Lewes, England

One day in the work of Rev David Powe, prison chaplain. Late September, 1995.

A little door in the huge prison gate opens to let me in at just after 8.15. I'm a trained vicar and I work in Lewes Remand Prison.

The reception office is busy as usual. They hand me my large bunch of keys, with a message pinned to them. Someone has phoned in the night. Apparently a prisoner's mother has died. I have to check out the story before I tell him. Last month I found out that one guy's grandfather had apparently 'died' four times! When I asked him about it he said, 'Well, you believe in the resurrection, don't you Padré?'

They think quickly, some of these people! Sure I do, but four times is a bit much!

'Jesus rose from the dead once and stayed alive for ever!' I told him firmly.

Doors clank and bang as I unlock, then lock them again after me. They come in sets of two – one with bars of metal, the other solid wood. By nine o'clock, I'm in my office, opening the post. Six letters come from people who have heard about what is going on here. Radio stations, magazines and newspapers have told the story of how, over the seventeen months I've spent as full-time chaplain here, 389 prisoners have become Christians. Those kind of numbers are unusual, and people write to say it's great to hear some good news for once!

One note reads,

'Dear David, You won't know me, but my name's Joel and I'm 13 years old. I saw what's happening in a magazine and I think it's great. But some of the prisoners don't have a Bible. I have two, so I'm sending you this for someone.'

I'll pass Joel's Bible on to Paul, who became a Christian a few days back. It will cheer him up. The authorities are sending him to a special hospital and he's upset about leaving us.

I take a quick look at the other letters and messages on the answer-phone. My secretary, Jackie, will be able to deal with them. Things are happening so fast now that I don't know what I'd do without Jackie. She has worked for me since last June. Local Christians raise the money to pay her wages.

I'm now free to go to F wing, where the convicted prisoners are. Lewes is a 'local remand prison' for people from this area who are accused of a crime and have to wait in prison for their trials. F wing prisoners are different. They have already been tried, found guilty and given short sentences – up to two years in jail. That means I have plenty of time to work with them. Around three quarters have become Christians.

I've only been on F wing a few seconds and people are queueing to see me. Mike is first. He calls me to one side. 'Can you say some prayers for my old mate Dan?' he says. 'He noticed I was different since he last saw me, so I told him, "Yeah, I have changed. I've become a Christian, mate!" Dan laughed and called me a few things, but I don't care. I'm praying for him!'

'Great! I'll look out for him,' I promise. The criminals who live in an area often know each other well. When they come in here and spend hours each day with an old friend who has changed, well, they want to know why.

Then it's back to the queue. I never know what prisoners are going to call me, or what they will ask.

'Father, could you get me a special visit?'

'My cell mate's down in the dumps. I think he needs your special touch, Vicar.'

"Ere, Sky Pilot, you believe in God. How come my daughter's got cancer?'

Many of these men know nothing about church or God, and they have some big problems. I can't help them much – only Jesus will do that, so I always turn the conversation round to him.

'Can I have a radio, Your Worship?' a new prisoner asks me.

'What's your name?' I ask. Jesus always called people by name.

'Steve.'

'Where's your room, Steve? Shall we go and have a talk?' I call it a room, not a cell. Jesus treated everyone like they were worth something. OK, some of these people are in prison because they have done bad things, but haven't we all? Jesus said that if you think angry thoughts about someone it's as bad as murdering them. If that's true, the only reason I'm not a prisoner is because I've not been caught yet!

'What are you doing in here, then?' I ask Steve,

on the way. He tells me. It's not good news.

'OK Steve,' I say, once we are in his room, 'it's like this. Only God can sort your life out. Do you want God or not?'

'God? I didn't realise he was still hanging around!'

Most people I ask say sure they would like God to help them. They wonder why no one ever told them he was interested in them before. Others yell, 'Push off!' – only not so politely! These men can have twenty years of terrible violence behind them. I know they'd stab me in the eye with a biro as soon as look at me. People think it's easy for a chaplain to be up-front in prison, but it's not. There are some hard men here. I have to make myself think of St Paul's words, 'I'm doomed if I don't preach the Gospel.' I could enjoy a much quieter life either staying in my office, or talking about the weather!

Steve decides he wants to become a Christian. He tells God he's sorry and asks Jesus to be the new boss of his life. I pray for him.

'Hey,' he says, 'you didn't tell me I'd feel like I'd been lit up by a light-bulb. It's better than crack!'

'Howard, meet Steve!' I introduce him to a Christian orderly who works on the wing. Howard will help Steve get to know Jesus a bit more and give him a radio, a Walkman and part of the Bible on tape. Like many of the prisoners, Steve can't read or write, so a printed Bible won't help. We gave one once to a hard nut called David, who became a Christian. He got his cell-mate, Mark, to read him a chapter out loud every night.

'How did you get Mark to do that?' I asked.

'Told him I'd beat him up if he didn't!' David replied. Fortunately, Mark came to know Jesus for himself shortly afterwards!

Right now Howard is welcoming Steve to God's family, which leaves me free to talk to a few more men on the wing. Later, back in the office, I tell Jackie about Steve. She phones a local church who pray for all our new Christians. One of them will write to Steve by tomorrow and a Christian volunteer who helps in the prison will get him involved in daily Bible studies, either on the wing or in the chapel.

Then I'm off to another wing. I try to make sure each part of the prison gets a visit from myself or from one of our three part-time chaplains every day. There's the hospital wing, the punishment block, the special wing where sex offenders are kept separate from the rest of the prisoners – for their own safety – and B wing for young offenders. Seventeen years old, many of them are, and hooked on drugs or alcohol. There are four or five to a cell, so it's tough for them to read the Bible or say they want to follow Jesus. The others give them a hard time and they can't get away or escape off by themselves. The officers are watching them, even while they sleep.

But now I'm on A wing, seeing prisoners who have not been tried yet. Some only stay here for a few days, which is why I believe in wasting no time before asking if they want Jesus to change their lives.

Kev says he wants a word with me. He became a Christian shortly after he arrived here last week. Back in his room he tells me he's going to plead guilty at his trial.

'And I'm gonna tell them that all that xxxxing money in my flat was from selling xxxxing drugs.'

Every time Kev opens his mouth, swear words

tumble out. He has always spoken like that and I can't expect him to stop overnight. He is changing in more important ways, though, like wanting to be truthful and to get his life straightened out.

'They could double your sentence, if you admit to crimes they don't even know about,' I warn him.

'I'll take the punishment for what I've done,' he said and grinned. 'I need a few years in prison to get straight. Once I'm out I wanna be ready to tell everyone about Jesus.'

We find that most who become Christians are honest about the crimes they have committed. Many write to people they have robbed or mugged, apologising.

Between 11.30 and 1.30 the prisoners are banged up in their cells. It's the officers' lunch hour and mine too, not that I find time to eat lunch, most days. I'd rather try to snatch a quick time of prayer with Jackie, or whoever is around. Things go better when I pray. I think it's because God guides me to the right people. I expect at least two to become Christians here every day now.

I don't think much would happen here without a lot of people praying, though. There's a great bunch which works all over the country called the Prison Fellowship. They pray for us and, when Christians are sent to other prisons, they look out for them. We also contact pray-ers by phone if things get tense and difficult here.

Most important of all, the prisoners themselves pray. They pray for their cell-mates and for officers, even the ones who give them a hard time and who think all this Jesus stuff is a load of rubbish. Many officers, though, see that it's calmer in parts of the prison where people have become

Christians. The men are too busy praying and getting to know their Bibles to cause trouble! Some officers have started asking prisoners to pray for them and their families.

At lunchtime I return to my office to find a few messages from people who are worried about their relatives in prison. It's not easy for them, but there's good news too: a girlfriend of one has phoned to say she has seen the change in him. She wants to find out more about this Jesus person.

Jackie and I sort through some of the parcels which have arrived from well-meaning Christians. We get all sorts: tapes of long sermons given years ago, books of complicated Christian teaching, old dusty Bibles. They go straight in the bin. We need modern Bibles with bright pictures on the front – there's so little colour in this place it's the least we can do. And we need money to buy tapes and Walkmans and radios for those who can't read. Some of them haven't owned anything nice for so long, you should see their faces when we give them something!

When I first came here I found a drab chapel, with wooden pews. Only about three prisoners ever came to services. We bought a red carpet and comfy, bright blue chairs and we put lots of posters up on the walls. There's nowhere like it in the whole prison. Around forty come to Sunday services these days and sing and talk about what God has done for them. You never know what's going to happen next, but it's real – and it makes most churches look boring!

In the afternoon I'm back on the wings again, but I can find myself talking anywhere. I met one prisoner when he was driving a dumper truck across the courtyard.

'I enjoyed your service, Sunday!' he said.

'I'm glad to hear it. Are you a Christian?'

'No!' he said, 'And you've only three days to get me – I'm out of here after that!'

Before I had time to reply he sped off in the truck, laughing, and I didn't even know his name.

Two days later I had a message that a prisoner's father had died suddenly. After checking out the story I went to see him. He turned out to be the man from the dumper truck.

'I'm sorry Jon, but I've some bad news for you.' I told him what had happened.

He put his head in his hands. 'You don't know what you're saying. Two of my brothers killed themselves this year; and you believe there's a God?'

I talked to him for a few moments about how Jesus died on the cross, taking all the world's suffering and evil upon himself. 'And because of that you can get to know him. He can start helping you put things right again.'

'They can't get much worse!' Jon said. 'But this Jesus – does he really want to save me?'

'Yes, he does. He cares, he even died for you!'

Right there and then Jon knelt on the floor of the cell. With tears in his eyes he told Jesus he was sorry for all he had done wrong and asked him for a new start.

'I feel so clean,' he said afterwards.

The other day I was speaking at a church and someone said to me that prisoners only become Christians because they are desperate. Well, the thief who was crucified next to Jesus was desperate too – and Jesus welcomed him. When men come into prison they lose everything – home, job, and often their wife or girlfriend as well as their freedom. Of course they're desperate. Jesus is the only really good news they are likely to get. I know some don't stick at following him – the Bible says that not everyone will. But lots do, and nearly every day I hear from those who are still going all out for Jesus in other prisons.

There are never enough hours in the day to do all I want here. Before I know it, I find it's time to go home – but I'll be back tomorrow!

(Everything here is true but some names are changed.)

You can find out more about how to help by writing to: Rev David Powe, Chaplain, HM Prison, Lewes, E Sussex;
or: Prison Fellowship England and Wales, PO Box 945, Chelmsford, Essex CM2 7PX.

Rachel Cooke, Romania

Abandoned to die!

Rachel almost choked at the smell. She and an Australian nurse called Marigold were being shown round room after room of the children's wards. Battered-looking cots were each shared by two or three children. Many lay in their own diarrhoea, which explained the terrible stench. Some stayed quite still, while others rocked to and fro, their skin covered with sores. Some had huge eyes, skinny limbs and swollen bellies, reminding Rachel of pictures of children starving in an African famine. But this was a hospital in Europe.

None of the children took any notice of the people passing by; in fact, several tried to hide. A few made odd, rather frightening noises, but most lay in eerie silence, which made Rachel uneasy every time she thought about it. She had never seen a hospital like this one: the hospital for infectious diseases in Constanta, Romania. All the children on these wards had Human Immuno-Deficient virus – HIV – which they caught when they were given blood transfusions shortly after their birth. The blood was infected and Rachel knew that all of them would die. There is no cure for HIV, which becomes AIDS and destroys people's defences against disease.

Rachel was used to nursing children with cancer and some of them had died. Even so, British hospitals were full of happy sounds and colour. They had plenty of equipment and pain-killing drugs to help the children. There were lots of people to nurse and love and care for them. Nothing had prepared her for Romania.

At dinner time three untrained nursing helpers called infirmières rushed around the cots with feeding bottles. Rachel noticed that they never touched any of the children or held the bottles for them. When one boy threw his out of the cot, the heavy glass smashed on the floor, but no one gave him another.

Rachel noticed one baby sucking frantically, but the level in the bottle never changed. She took a closer look. The hole in the teat had been made bigger, but something white was blocking it. Later she realised that the hospital had no milk. They used rice-water instead, mixed with lumps of white feta cheese, which sometimes blocked the holes in the teats. No wonder some of the babies were starving.

Rachel and Marigold were horrified to discover a dead baby in a cot with two live ones. The infirmière shrugged and only later removed the body. One child died here every other day and no one seemed to care.

This place is horrific, thought Rachel. And I've volunteered to work here for three months. Well, I simply can't do it. I want to go home – now! In tears that night she told Marigold how she was feeling. 'It's hopeless. I mean, where do we start?

We don't even speak the language – and how can we work with those cruel people!'

'They seemed incredibly hard!' agreed Marigold. 'I never imagined nurses could treat babies like that – snatching them up by their wrists, dropping them.'

'I suppose,' she continued slowly, 'when you think there were only three on duty looking after eighty babies and they have to clean the ward as well! Those infirmières work twelve hours a day and are paid next to nothing. They've no training, or drugs or equipment. Most of the children have been abandoned by their parents. They're going to die anyway. I guess some hospital staff have given up seeing them as human beings.'

'I don't think they understand anything about AIDS, either!' said Rachel. 'Did you notice how they tried not to touch the children? As if they were afraid they would catch it?'

'Well, that's one thing we could do – show them it's not like that!'

'And show them how to potty train and feed the children properly!'

They prayed that night, 'Lord, it all seems too much for two people to do. But if you have plans and you can work through us, then please do it, Lord.'

The next day Rachel picked up a tiny baby, with huge brown eyes. She managed to speak enough Romanian to ask the nurse his age and nearly dropped him with surprise at the reply. Two years old? He looked more like two weeks! She stroked his little face and hands as he fed and later she kept returning to baby Liviu. After a few days he gave her the very first smile of his life – and she smiled back. Even if he is dying in this terrible place, God made him, she thought. Liviu deserved to be loved by someone!

Rachel asked the head nurse if the children could be given a place to play, rather than being left in their cots all day.

'Children do not play in hospital!' the nurse had snapped in reply.

'God, please help her see that things could be better!' Rachel prayed, over and over again. She wrote home. 'Please pray that the nurses begin to care about these little ones.'

She and Marigold started praying in each room of the ward, 'Lord we want this to be your place and for your love to be here.' They decided to work at first with the children in just one room of the ward, to show the Romanian nurses how love and human contact could make a real difference. Soon the children there began to look up excitedly, holding their arms up for attention whenever an adult came near.

Rachel and Marigold were working twelve hour shifts, but every morning when they went on duty and every evening before they returned to their flat they made sure that each child on the whole ward had a kiss and a cuddle. 'This is our Hug Round,' they told the Romanian nurses, who began to see how the children were changing. The older ones no longer made frightening noises. Some were trying to talk. There was no doubt that something good was happening, but there was such a long way to go!

Exhausted after nursing dying children for twelve hours every day in the terrible conditions at the hospital, Rachel and Marigold found it hard going back to their flat. They never knew how many cockroaches they would have to kill, or whether they would have to fetch water because their tap had run dry again. Often they had to queue for hours for food, because the Romanian shops had so little.

'You know, I can't believe I'm doing this,' Rachel said to Marigold. 'It's not as if I'm the adventurous type. I love my home and family back in England. All I ever wanted to do was to get married and have six children.'

'Oh, the comfortable life!' laughed Marigold. 'If we wanted that we shouldn't have volunteered to work with World Vision.'

Rachel grinned. 'Not very comfortable here, is it? But I'm amazed that I'm coping with things. I thought I'd freak out! It has to be God, helping me, I s'pose!' They were drinking black coffee, because they had no milk and she pulled a face. 'You know, it's funny what you miss,' she said. 'I'd give anything for a digestive biscuit, right now!'

Marigold laughed. 'You need to learn to ask God for the little things as well as the big ones!'

'I can't ask God for a digestive biscuit!'

'Rachel, the Romanians have never heard of digestives. How else are you going to get one?'

Next morning an English couple arrived.

'We're from Eurovangelism, come to deliver 500 Romanian children's Bibles,' the man said.

The woman added, 'Last night the Lord told me to give you these.' Looking a little embarrassed she handed half a jumbo packet of digestive biscuits to Rachel. 'Sorry – I'd already eaten half of them!'

God cares so much, not only for the children, but for me, Rachel thought! It was as well that she was learning she could depend on God, for, not long after that, Marigold became ill and had to leave Romania.

World Vision came to discuss the future. 'You know, Rachel, we really need you to stay on. In fact we need you for longer than the three months which you originally agreed to work here.'

Rachel knew she had to stay, for the sake of the children, but found it hard now she had no one to talk to. She still could not understand the Romanian language properly and people seemed afraid to talk to foreigners, because Romania's last ruler had made them report all conversations to the Secret Police. A few church people were friendly, though, including the Pastor, and one elderly couple offered to do all Rachel's shopping, which saved her hours of queuing for food.

As Rachel got to know the elderly man who did her shopping, she realised that he adored children. 'Why don't you come to the hospital, Isaiah?' she asked him. 'You could read to them in Romanian. They'd love it!' At first Isaiah was frightened of catching AIDS, but soon he was coming to the hospital regularly. The children all called him Grandpa and wanted to hold his hand or sit on his knee.

Rachel had also begun bringing some of the older children to her flat at weekends, and then to Sunday School. Some mothers in the church were worried their own children might catch AIDS, but after the Pastor arranged for someone to teach them about the illness, several families began to foster children at weekends. Most of the children on the AIDS ward had come from orphanages and had never been in an ordinary home, never felt part of a family or special to anyone. Now some had families of their own who loved them, helped them, and prayed for them as well!

People in England helped too. Rachel's brother had started an organisation called Operation Christmas Child (OCC) which brought supplies to the desperate people of Romania and other places. Soon after arriving in Constanta, Rachel asked for his help. First OCC sent milk, pain-killers, nappies and other things which made life more bearable for the children. Then Rachel asked if he would send them some boxes which British school children had filled with presents and food.

The Romanian nurses smiled at the delight on the children's faces when they opened the boxes. They found perhaps a little cuddly toy, a packet of sweets – and something different to eat. None of them had ever had presents before.

The hardest lesson for Rachel came one Christmas, when the lorry from OCC could not reach Constanta because of heavy snow. Most of the children had never known that Christmas Day was different from any other. Rachel so wanted this Christmas to be special for them, but now the presents would not arrive in time!

She knew she had to do something and thought of some woollen dolls she had kept back from the last delivery. On Christmas Eve she wandered the streets, wondering what else she could give the children. She managed to buy enough Romanian chocolate to give each child a small piece. It tasted horribly bitter. Then she saw some oranges for sale, which was very unusual in Constanta. They were expensive, but she bought some.

That night she fretted that these were poor gifts for children who might never live to see another Christmas. She could imagine such presents being thrown to one side in disgust back in England. But the children in Constanta hospital had never known a Christmas morning like that one. They hugged the dolls and pounced on the chocolate and oranges – the first they had ever seen. Soon even the Romanian nurses were busy helping them peel the fruit and laughing with them.

Not long afterwards, Rachel had to leave the area for a short while. When she returned, she found that a nurse had baked one boy a cake for his birthday and all the children had made hats. They were having a party. The children were not quite sure what was happening at first, as most of them had never heard of birthdays before. After that the nurses decided to go on having parties, though they could not manage a separate one for each child. Instead they arranged birthday celebrations once a month, with proper food – chicken and chips and cake – and a present for everyone.

The nurses were certainly changing. Not only had they thought of arranging parties, but Rachel found out that they had begun to give money out of their meagre earnings, so that the children who died could have some kind of funeral. Then the same head nurse who had been so against children playing in hospital took it on herself to make a play area for the children on the ward. Operation Christmas Child supplied the toys.

After three years working in Romania Rachel could hardly believe this was the same ward she had seen at the beginning. Two of the staff had decided to follow Jesus and she felt so sad to be leaving them, the other nurses and the children. Before Rachel went home, the doctor in charge of the ward asked her for one more thing.

'Do you think your brother could build us a home, like the one he built in Cluj?'

The doctor had been there on a visit. It was a proper home, where children could live, not in a hospital ward or orphanage, but in a family. Rachel promised to ask, though she knew that it would cost a great deal of money.

After she returned to England, Rachel was surprised to be awarded a Heart of Gold. When Esther Rantzen asked her in front of the television cameras what she most wanted, she said, 'A home for the children, so they can all have a mum and a dad.' People all over Britain responded most generously and a home for ten of the children is now being built by the side of a beautiful lake in Constanta. Two Romanian Christian houseparents will be trained in how to care for children with AIDS and the children will live in this loving family with them for the rest of their short lives.

'I felt I couldn't do much,' said Rachel. 'But I was there and I saw so many of my prayers answered. I saw Jesus work a miracle in that hospital!'

To find out how you can help, write to:
Operation Christmas Child, PO Box 732, Wrexham, Clwyd LL11 1RQ;
or: World Vision UK, 559 Avebury Boulevard, Milton Keynes, Buckinghamshire, MK9 3PG.

Dr Paul Raj – India

Life or death?

'You have elephantiasis,' the doctor told Paul. 'There's no cure. It's possible an operation might help but, if anything goes wrong, you might never be able to speak again!'

Paul needed his voice in his job: teaching philosophy at an Indian university. He was still a young man and he did not know what to do. The illness had made his neck swell until it was bigger than his head.

Then, one day in 1970, the University's Professor of English told Paul about a Christian meeting in Bombay. 'A Canadian man is praying for people to be healed,' he said.

Paul did not believe in that kind of thing. He had been brought up in a strict Hindu family and, though most of what he was now teaching had to do with the Hindu religion, secretly Paul was no longer sure that the gods existed. And if they did, why should they have anything to do with people?

Religion seemed to cause people nothing but trouble. Paul began to have doubts about it while still at school. His parents were furious because he dared to touch one of his classmates who was of a lower 'caste'. According to Hinduism everyone is born into one caste or another. Paul and his family were Brahmins – the highest caste - but some people were born so low in the system that they were considered 'untouchable'. What kind of god would want to treat people like that, Paul wondered? No, everyone would get on much better without religion.

But now a senior professor was asking him to go to a religious meeting. Not wanting to offend him, Paul said simply, 'Sorry, I cannot go.'

The next day the Professor handed him an envelope containing a large sum of money. He obviously thought that Paul had turned down his invitation because he could not afford the train fare to Bombay. He really cares about me, Paul thought. He's a well-educated man. If he reckons it's worth risking so much money, maybe I should go!

After a long train journey he arrived. When the meeting ended he gave a letter from the Professor to the Canadian, who read it, looked Paul up and down twice, then said, 'You've come to the wrong person. I'm not a healer. I never healed anyone.'

Paul could not believe it. 'Then why did the Professor send me to you?' he spluttered.

'Ask him, not me! But I can see your neck's bad. I'll give you the name of someone who might help.'

What a waste of time, Paul thought, but the man was already writing. On a piece of paper he printed: *Jesus Christ, Son of God.*

'Very funny!' Paul spat out the words. 'You think I'm about to die and go to heaven!' He had rarely felt so angry.

The Canadian smiled. 'Come now, you've travelled all this way to see me – but I'm only a man. If doctors can't cure you, how could I? I'm going to die one day, like everyone else! But there is one who is always alive. Trust in Jesus. Only he can heal you!'

Paul knelt down. The Canadian prayed for him, then gave Paul a Bible and told him to go home.

During the two days' train journey, Paul's neck gradually shrank to the right size again. When his mother insisted on taking him to the doctor who had been treating him, the doctor refused to believe he was the same person. 'Impossible for the swelling to disappear,' he said. 'You've brought me his twin brother!'

But Paul had no twin brother and he had to admit that something very strange had happened. Maybe this Christian God did have unseen powers! He started to read the Bible and learnt about the history of a people called the Jews. But what did that have to do with him?

'Read it again!' advised the Professor.

Paul read the whole Bible for a second time, but still it made no sense to him.

'Then wait for the Spirit of God to show Jesus to you!' the Professor said.

A few weeks later, while he was teaching at the University, Paul received some terrible news. His youngest brother had died very suddenly. Paul rushed home. When he kissed his seven year old brother goodbye that morning he had seemed fine, yet now a tropical disease had killed him. In his room that night, Paul could not sleep. Is this what human life is all about, he thought? Is this the end? My favourite brother – I loved him so much!

Then, as all these thoughts were churning around in his mind, a verse from the Bible came to him, clear and beautiful: '*Though I walk through the valley of the shadow of death, you are with me.*' If death is a shadow, thought Paul, there must be a light beyond. Suddenly he knew: Jesus was that light. Being human was not enough. Jesus died so that Paul, and anyone else who trusted him, might find real life. Jesus rose for them, and would come back for them. Paul ran outside and the night sky seemed incredibly wonderful. This Jesus cared about people; he could follow a God like that!

When he told his mother that he had become a Christian she said, 'Impossible!' To become a Christian placed you in an 'untouchable' caste and no one would marry the relation of an untouchable. Didn't Paul realise that he would bring disgrace on the family and that his sisters could never marry?

When he would not give up on Jesus, his family, who had always loved and cared for him, disowned Paul and threw him out of the house. People at the University said that his brother's death had turned him mad. Paul felt so alone, until he read in the Bible: *'Even your mother may forget you, but I will never leave you.'* He knew he would go on living for Jesus, whatever that might mean.

Jesus cares for everyone!

After he became a Christian and was turned out of his home, Paul went to stay with a well-known American missionary called Stanley Jones. He learnt so much about his new-found faith from this man. Soon Paul felt that God was asking him to go and tell other people the good news about Jesus.

'Then go to people who have not heard before,' Stanley advised him.

Paul studied maps of India. There seemed to be Christian churches everywhere, but the old missionary pointed out an area in the middle of south-east India. 'It's thick forest, without proper roads. Ten million people live there. They can't read or write and no one has ever told them about Jesus.'

The best way into the area was by boat, so in September 1971, Paul caught a motor launch up the river Godavari. He did not know that Naxelite Communists used the forest as a hiding place and that some of them were terrorists. The local police kept a sharp lookout for any strangers and they soon spotted Paul. He was arrested and taken to the city of Bhadrachalam.

'Where is your Communist group based?' the police asked him.

'I'm not from any group. I've simply come to tell the people about Jesus.'

The police did not believe him and he had no proof except for his Bible. The men started to beat him.

'Why are you doing this?' Paul shouted.

'Listen to him! Only a trained terrorist would be so arrogant! Tell us where you come from, or else!'

After that Paul kept silent. The police imprisoned him and beat him whenever they felt like it, but this made Paul even more determined to tell the forest people about Jesus. After two months his parents found out what had happened and convinced the police that Paul was no Communist.

As soon as he was set free, Paul set off again up the Godavari river until he reached a place called Kunavaram. From there he walked through the forest until he found a village. He carried a hand microphone slung over one shoulder and a battery pack to power it on the other. He switched on the microphone and blew into it. Terrified at the strange noise, the people ran away up trees, or hid in bushes.

By evening their curiosity brought them back and some even dared to touch Paul's clothes, which seemed strange to them. They themselves wore little or nothing and spoke a tribal language called Koya, which Paul did not at first understand. As the months went by he learnt enough words to start telling them about Jesus' love.

He travelled around, spending a few nights in one village, then moving on to another. Sometimes villagers would invite him to stay in one of their thatched mud huts; otherwise he would sleep out in the open. Even at night it was always warm enough, but poisonous snakes were a real danger and once he woke to see a tiger, only a few metres away. Its teeth were tearing into a deer which it had just caught. Paul felt thankful that it had not found him.

Once he became extremely sick with typhoid fever, which kills many Indians every year. After he had been ill for a fortnight, a villager took him to a small police outpost and left him on the veranda. When the policemen found him they decided to let him stay there because he was bound to die in a day or two. 'Then you can bury him,' Paul heard the man in charge say.

Every few hours a policeman would come and look at Paul to see if he had died. Paul felt he had to moan or make some noise, or they might bury him then and there. By the following day he had no energy left to groan and knew that he was dying. He prayed silently in the words of Psalm 103: *'Bless the Lord, my soul, and don't forget all that he has done for you.*' Then he closed his eyes, expecting to wake up in heaven.

Meanwhile an engineer, who had been helping build a dam nearby, called at the police outpost to ask about something. 'Why is that young man lying on the mat?' he wanted to know. He recognised Paul. As children they had sat on the same bench together, in a school hundreds of kilometres away! He carried his old classmate back to his own jeep and made sure that Paul received the right medicines.

As Paul began to feel better, he kept thinking about the verse from Psalm 23 which had been so special to him when he first put his trust in Jesus, *'Though I walk through the valley of the shadow of death, you are with me.'* How amazing that his old friend should have arrived in that far-away place just then. God really had looked after him – right up to the point of death!

When he was well enough to return to the forest, Paul started to pray for people who were sick. He would then move on and visit several more villages. By the time he returned to the first, many of the people he had prayed for were cured. Then, when he told them about the power and love of Jesus, they believed him. They were simple people and really trusted Jesus. When their lives changed their friends sat up and took notice, and more people became Christians.

It began slowly. By 1976 there was a small church of seven families meeting in a village called Gangolu, but Paul realised that people in the area had new problems, which Jesus cared about too. Around that time, the mid 1970s, outsiders started coming to the forest and offered the people a few coins to persuade them to sign pieces of paper. The forest people could not read, so they did not understand that the papers said that they no longer owned the land which had once been theirs. They had lost any right to decide what happened there and could only watch as the outsiders cut down great areas of forest for timber, or to farm the land.

Where the forest had gone, the local people could no longer hunt or gather food to eat. Worse things followed. When the heavy monsoon rains fell every year, the forest used to absorb the water, letting it into the rivers gradually. Now it all rushed down at once, causing floods which destroyed whole areas. Then the outsiders started building factories and mining and polluted the water which the forest people used to drink.

Outsiders acted as though the tribal people did not count. They saw them as lower than even the 'untouchable' castes: more like forest animals than people. Paul, though, knew that Jesus cared for the forest people as much as for anyone else. He realised that unless they learnt to read and write and stand up for themselves, others would go on taking away their land and their ways of staying alive.

Paul began to set up schools. Today his organisation runs six of them, with 700 pupils altogether and a college which teaches older girls and women skills like sewing, so that they can earn money to live on once more.

Paul also worried that many forest people died needlessly because they had so little medical care. Today, trained people from his churches run village clinics in a special van, which some Christians in Germany helped them buy.

Paul started all on his own but now has eighty people working full-time with him. 60,000 adults and children meet in 350 village churches. He is still not satisfied, though. 'Jesus cares for all ten million of these people – and so few know the good news about him for themselves!' he says, as he turns once again to his work.

To find out more, write to:
Pioneer India, 20 Clinton Avenue, East Molesey, Surrey, KT8 0HS.

Jenny Sinnadurai – working among Tamil peoples

'I need 50 cents for the bus fare, God,' Jenny said, sitting down for a rest by the side of the road. She felt so faint, having left home at six in the morning and walked the ten kilometres to church, all by herself, as she did every Sunday. Now, after the service, she was returning in the hottest part of the day. There was nothing unusual about that, but today the twelve-year-old could go no further.

Hang on – what was that, shining in the gutter? A coin. She picked it up and smiled. Being the only Christian in her village wasn't easy, but when God helped her in difficult times, it proved he was real and her faith in him grew.

It had all started the year before. 'Would you like to come to the esplanade with me?' Jenny's mum asked her. 'They say there's an American doing miracles there!'

'Yes please, Mum!' replied Jenny at once. They sold ice cream down at Jaffna's esplanade. Mum was bound to buy her some!

They lived close to Jaffna, a big town in the north of Sri Lanka. At the esplanade they found over 3000 people singing some beautiful songs – and then a man started preaching, in English. Even though the preacher's words were translated into her own Tamil language, she found them hard to follow. She only really understood one little bit, right at the end. 'You can be born again – today!'

Her mother, noticing she had disappeared, thought she had gone to buy some ice cream. In fact Jenny had rushed to the front of the meeting to join the people asking for prayer.

'What is it you want, dear?' the translator said.

'Born again!' she replied. Her father followed the Hindu religion, while her mother did not believe in any gods. Jenny only knew that her life was a mess. She had been living without God, and she had to get to know him. When the preacher prayed for her, she heard another voice, inside her, say, 'I will use you more powerfully than this man.' Though surprised, she felt so happy. She had found God! He loved her and had plans for her life!

That day marked a complete change for Jenny. She had no Bible, but she knew Jesus and realised that he did not like her doing certain things, for example, she used to tell fortunes. People kept asking her to do it, because what she said always seemed to come true. Now, though, she sensed that God saw fortune-telling as wrong, so she stopped. Eventually she found a church where she could learn from other Christians and the Bible.

When Jenny grew up and left school she started working as a nurse. In her spare time she ran the church youth club but they would not let her do much else, because Tamil women are not normally leaders.

Her father paid for all his four children to have a good education, but he got into debt. Men kept coming to the door and shouting that he owed them money. Jenny hated to see him so unhappy. Perhaps she could find a job abroad? She would earn far more than she could in Sri Lanka and send money back home.

She found a hospital job in an Arab country and before long she had paid off her father's debt. Other Sri Lankans worked there, and Jenny invited some of them round to her home to pray. Very soon, twenty had become Christians, but all this time Jenny had something nagging at the back of her mind. She sensed that God was asking her to go to England.

She was enjoying a good life, with a lovely home, an interesting job and all the money she could possibly want. Why should she give it up? She made excuses to God: she did not speak English well and anyway didn't the twenty new Christians need her? They had no church to go to.

Then, one day, Jenny's breast began to hurt and soon the pain became so bad that she had to visit the doctor. After some tests he told her, 'Cancer, I'm afraid. We could operate, but we think it has already spread to other parts of your body.'

'How long do I have to live, doctor?'

'About three months.'

Jenny had never felt so frightened. Her work in the hospital had to do with examining tests for cancer. She happened to see her own results, but, instead of passing them on to another doctor so she could have treatment, she tore them up.

'OK, God,' she said, 'I've had a good life here, but I won't enjoy it if I'm dead. I'm sorry I wouldn't go to England! If you still want me to serve you there, I will – but you'll have to save my life first!'

Jenny stayed at home and prayed. The pain became unbearable and her body swelled so much that she could not do up her clothes. Only after two weeks did she begin to feel a little better. In three months, the very time the doctor predicted she would die, she was completely well again.

She returned to work in the hospital and kept asking God about how exactly she should go to England. One day her boss suggested she should train for a higher qualification. 'There's a good course in England,' he said. So Jenny's employers paid her fare to London.

Jenny felt very shy and alone when she arrived in London. She found a church and sat quietly in the back row. Part way through the service the preacher walked right down the church and spoke to Jenny. 'God has brought you here for a great purpose,' he prophesied. 'He will raise you up and use you in many nations.'

Timid little Jenny could hardly believe that this was happening to her! Even a year later, when Pastor Adrian Hawkes wanted to welcome her as a church member, she refused to go forward in a service. 'I can't stand up in front of all those people!' she said.

If the preacher's words were true, though, Jenny realised she needed training at Bible college, not in medicine. She wrote to her bosses, who replied that they understood about her leaving the hospital course and even sent £3,500 which they said they owed from her pension.

With her own Tamil people she felt less scared. She had met some in London and helped several to become Christians. They started meeting together.

By 1985 Jenny's brother had moved to Paris, France, and he invited her to spend Christmas with him. He lived in a flat with seven other Tamils and Jenny started telling them about Jesus and all that he had done for her. Soon all eight were in tears, including her brother. 'We want to know this Jesus!' they said.

After they met him for themselves they were so excited that they invited more friends round next day.

Wonderful, thought Jenny afterwards, but what am I to do with these twenty new Christians when I live so far away? Churches nearby did not seem to want them, so she phoned Adrian, back in London.

'Oh my nerves!' he said. What had shy little Jenny done now? 'Well, you can't just leave them,' he told her. 'You'll have to keep visiting Paris to teach and train them.'

At that time Jenny worked every morning in a nursery school plus three nights a week in an old people's home and she spent the afternoons studying at Bible College. Now she started to go to Paris once a week as well! After Friday's Bible lessons finished she would catch a coach to Paris. On Saturday she led a Bible study for the group of new Christians and a service on the Sunday. She caught the overnight coach back to England, and went straight to the nursery school to begin work at 8am.

When her brother had learnt enough about his new faith to run the group once a week, Jenny cut her visits to one a month. Then, after a year, one Tamil woman in the group caught a serious illness called TB (tuberculosis). When Jenny prayed, God healed her and the woman told her family what had happened. Her sister lived in Switzerland and had a three year old daughter who could not hear or speak.

'Could your friend Jenny pray for my daughter?' she asked.

'Give the phone to the child,' Jenny said. As she was praying down the telephone, suddenly the little girl said, 'Mum' and 'Dad' – the first words she had ever spoken. She could hear perfectly!

Her parents were thrilled and so keen to meet Jenny that they sent her air fare to Switzerland. She introduced them to Jesus, along with eight of their friends. They invited her back to take a meeting the next week and 125 people came. Soon Jenny had a small church in Switzerland as well as in France. Most people in both had fled from fighting between Tamil and Singhalese tribes in Sri Lanka and had come to Europe as refugees. Huge camps housed many who felt very lost and alone. Jenny longed for more of them to find Jesus, and new friends and 'family' in the church.

'I need someone to help me,' she told God, and in 1988 along came Karen, from New Zealand. She had been travelling around the world, sightseeing and then working as a nurse whenever she needed more money. She loved travel, music and organising things and she had always felt that God wanted her to work outside her own country. Jenny needed someone to organise things for her and to train worship leaders for the new church meetings. When Karen came to see what was going on, they both understood how they fitted into God's plan together.

They started leading teams into the Swiss camps, where newly arrived refugees had to stay until they learnt German and found a job. The refugees came to Jenny's church on Sundays, just to be with other Tamils. Many became Christians and their lives changed dramatically.

Most of them were young men who had run away from Sri Lanka because there was a high chance they would be forced to join either the

Singhalese army or one of the Tamil guerilla groups. Franklin was one of these. Though he loved fighting, he would not join either side, and he only escaped being shot for his refusal because someone recognised his name and helped him get away. He found work on a ship but he was always drunk and everyone knew that when they arrived in port he would be the first to start a fight.

When Franklin found his way to Switzerland he knew no one and accepted Jenny's invitation to come to church only because he wanted to meet other Tamils. When he arrived in the meeting everyone was worried because they could see he was drunk and had heard about the fights he started. But he became a Christian that day and within a week had given up drinking, smoking and violence. Today he leads a Tamil church.

Several new Christians had done terrible things in Sri Lanka: others had seen dreadful things happen to those they loved. The church helped in practical ways such as finding them jobs and somewhere to live outside the camps. Even more importantly the church became like a new family to them, praying for and loving them.

God kept his promise to small, shy young Jenny. He did raise her up and use her in many nations, as Adrian had prophesied. He gave her the boldness to start churches among a people that did not believe in woman leaders. Today she travels for him to many countries of the world and speaks to thousands of people. It is amazing what God can do!

You can find out more by writing to: Jenny Sinnadurai, c/o Rainbow Churches, PO Box 1908, Seven Sisters Road, London N4 3PY.

Steve Neale – London

We need a Combine Harvester!

Steve was reading a book about the place where he lives in south-east London. 'Hey, it says here that 1500 children used to go to the Baptist Sunday School just down the road!' he exclaimed to his wife. 'Apparently, the police had to direct the traffic each week so they could all cross the road – and that was just the crowd from one church!'

Steve was a warehouse manager who, in his spare time, worked with children in his own church. He enjoyed seeing them learn to follow Jesus through something the church called KEY groups – which stands for Kingdom Evangelism for Youngsters.

KEY groups had two main aims – to show that God loves children and wants them to know him and that he has a job for each one to do. The church believed children needed training to serve God in different ways just as much as adults do.

Once the KEY groups were working well Steve started asking, 'What about the kids who never go to church?' He had read that, earlier this century, eighty-five out of every hundred children attended church or Sunday School. In the 1990s the same number – eighty-five out of every hundred – never went near church at all.

'It's not just going to church that matters,' Steve complained to his wife, Achanda. 'I've been reading about John Wesley. Back in the 1700s he would tell all these children about Jesus – 900 or 1000 at a time – and they really caught something. They'd get together to pray for people. If churches didn't make them welcome, they went up in the hills in groups of twenty or thirty and worshipped God there, despite the cold. And you know, those children went back home and told the adults about Jesus. Sometimes everyone who lived in a village would start crying and asking Jesus to save them!'

'So what are we missing now?' Achanda asked.

'I don't know. It's not as if the children I speak to are against Jesus!' Many who never went near a church had told Steve that they prayed and wanted to follow Jesus – though no one had shown them how. 'But most get discouraged and give up after a while,' Steve said.

'We've seen children become Christians!' Achanda pointed out.

'Yes, but I believe that God is asking us to gather in a big harvest right now.' After a moment, Steve continued, 'It's like we're using a pair of scissors to cut the crop on a huge field. To do the job properly, though, we need a combine harvester!'

Each year, in the school holidays, Steve's church ran a Bible club with all kinds of games and activities. Lots of children came, though they never went to anything else run by a church.

At the end of the first day of 1991's holiday

club, Steve challenged the children, 'Stand up if you want to follow Jesus.' One or two brave ones did just that. Then three twelve year old lads also stood up. They were hard, gang-leader types who had been messing around all morning. Most of the other children were scared of them.

'We're not going to follow Jesus,' one of them said. 'We follow Satan!' And the three of them walked out.

They did not return the next day, but showed up again at the final session.

'Stand now if you want to follow Jesus!' Steve said, once again.

The three of them looked at one another – and then, slowly, they stood.

'You really want to follow Jesus?' Steve asked.

'Yeah! Yeah, we do!'

It was not easy for them to change their minds like that, in front of all the others, Steve realised. By now many more children were on their feet, having decided they would follow Jesus as well.

Steve's team felt so happy. They invited all of them to come with their parents to the church the next Sunday morning – and told the children there would be fun and games and party food. When not one of them came, Steve realised that they still felt uneasy about church. After all, no one they knew ever went there. The team felt sad as, slowly, they lost contact with all the children.

Steve began praying hard and also started reading a book called *Streets of Pain*, by Bill Wilson, an American who lived in Brooklyn, a very poor area of New York. People there were likely to die even younger than someone from a really poor country like Bangladesh. Bill ran a children's church and 14,000 children came every week. Their parents could be drug addicts, criminals – even murderers. Yet many of the children saw God work miracles in their lives and in their families. It seemed as if the whole area was beginning to change.

This is what I've been looking for, thought Steve. He knew he had to go and see it for himself. Before long, there he was – in New York one Saturday – watching fifty buses ferry three different lots of children to Bill's Metro Church. Steve noticed bullet holes in the windows of one or two of the church buses – where people had shot at them! Yet in the meeting the children listened quietly, joining in well – and they really worshipped God. Teachers from the rowdy schools of the area, visiting Metro Church, could not understand how it was so calm.

Steve heard story after story of how children had prayed for their families and how Jesus helped them put their messed-up lives straight. He asked Bill's team, 'What's your secret?'

'We have a four point plan,' one of the leaders explained. 'First we take church out to where the kids are. We do meetings and games on the streets. Second, once we've made contact we visit the children every week, and invite them along here. That means their families get to know us. Third, the children would never come on their own, so we collect them in buses and, fourth, our meetings are planned especially for these particular kids. They wouldn't get on with a normal church service or Sunday School!'

'Sounds amazing!' said Steve.

'Sure is! But it takes real hard work. We've been going for years, building it up, and now we're beginning to see Brooklyn changing. Government money is coming in and good things are happening! It's been tough – I've been shot at and beaten up – but it's sure worth it!'

Back home Steve talked to the leaders of his church, which had congregations on different estates in south-east London. They had tried to get to know their neighbours and tell them about Jesus, but often found it hard going.

'Suppose we get a truck and do clubs on the streets of those estates?' Steve enthused. 'The Christians who live there could visit the children afterwards and invite them to a children's church. We could run it like the one in New York!'

'What would you call it?'

'Popcorn!' Steve replied. 'Because I believe this idea is going to work like our combine harvester. Then, once we've gathered in the corn, something amazing's going to happen to it. God'll get hold of children and they'll jump around and grow really fast – just like corn popping.'

'Well ... perhaps ...'

'Anyway, I like popcorn – and so do most kids I know!'

That settled it. By then Steve was working full time for the church. He got together a team which started Popcorn Children's Church in July 1994. They bought an old Leyland van which used to belong to British Telecom. The team set to work making flaps and hinges, so, after they had driven somewhere, they could open the back and it became a mobile stage.

Five congregations from different estates said they would like to give Popcorn a go and the team spent four days in each. On the first day,

Christians walked around the estate, praying. On the second day they brought a PA system, with clowns and banners and lots of noise to attract everyone's attention. Then the team knocked on up to 1000 doors, inviting the children to a one hour holiday club on their estate.

On the third and fourth days the truck arrived and set up anywhere they found enough space. Then the children registered in either red or yellow team. Each had a sticker, which they swapped at the end of the morning for a chocolate bar – or some popcorn!

The club's programme moved fast, starting with games led from the front and some lively, aerobic-type dancing which everyone joined in. Then they sat and listened to Ralph the Dog, a puppet who was always getting into trouble of one kind or another. In 'tell us' time, children could speak into the microphone about their new skateboard or the fact their cat was sick. Then they had a chance to pray into the mike. 'I hope my Gran gets better soon,' or 'Please help Sam who's being bullied!'

Finally, one of the leaders gave a very short talk and afterwards asked God to show them that what he said was real. Early on Steve's main point was that God loved each one of them. He prayed, 'Come and show these children that you love them. Speak to them, give them a hug!' One boy put up his hand and said he could see a donkey in his mind's eye. Bit odd, Steve thought!

Then a girl said, 'I can see people running around with long branches in their hands.'

Another boy added, 'They're saying, "Jesus is coming!"'

Steve saw that God was showing these children

what happened when Jesus went to Jerusalem on Palm Sunday. Realising that they had not heard the story before, he told them all about it – and the children were amazed. God had started telling one of his true stories directly to them! They felt very special.

This is what we want, thought Steve. It's a great story on its own, but when God uses it to show children he is real – that's something else! Lives are going to change!

At the end of each two-day club, many children on the estate wanted to follow Jesus. Someone from the congregation would visit them each week, inviting them to Popcorn Children's church on a Saturday morning. The children's parents got to know these regular visitors and friendships grew. Often the Christians could help in some way, like doing a bit of shopping if Mum was ill. They also organised fun events like fireworks parties, or outings to the sea for the whole family. People on the estates began to see that these Christians were good news.

Buses brought the children to Popcorn on Saturday mornings. Steve realised that most 10-14 year olds preferred to be doing things, so they became the helpers, and the programme was aimed at 5-10 year olds. The band were also 10-14s. All of them enjoyed playing at Popcorn, they practised hard – and they were good. Most adults thought it was too loud but the children loved it!

Soon the children were praying for one another – and seeing their prayers answered. Once Steve asked them to write down what had happened. One girl wrote, 'When we were praying I felt God's hand on my shoulder and he said, "Don't doubt, I can touch you!" A few days afterwards

Mum took me to hospital. You see, my kidneys have always been tiny. They only worked a fifth as well as they should and I needed to see the doctor quite often. But this time he couldn't believe it. My kidneys had grown to full size. They were working perfectly!'

An eight year old boy stood up in the 'tell us' time. 'God's told me that he is my father. Even though my dad has died, God will never leave me!' he said. The team found out that, not only had this boy's father died – his mother, too, was seriously ill. Later she died as well. Afterwards the boy said, 'God kept his promise – and he's holding me really close.'

Two sisters stood and explained that they didn't have a dad. 'Our mum works really hard, but last Thursday she hurt her back and the doctor said she had to stay in bed for two weeks. So we put our hands on her and asked Jesus to make her better.' Straightaway their mother was healed!

Popcorn was growing. After just a year about 260 children would turn up in any one week and Popcorn was keeping in touch with 650 children altogether. There are all sorts of reasons why not everyone can come every week – for example many children are visiting a parent who has left home.

News of Popcorn spread as team members talked in school assemblies and invited the children along. Also, the truck took clubs to different estates from time to time. On one estate, an eleven-year-old girl stood up and told everyone how her house was burnt down. 'People set fire to it, because me and my family are black,' she said. 'But the good thing is – I got to know Jesus a few weeks before it happened. He's looked after me all the way through!'

On the same estate, some rough types in their early twenties started throwing water bombs at the team – and they had put pieces of lead in them! The children who had come with the team hid behind the truck and prayed – and the trouble-makers left. Then a twelve year old lad stood up and said how Jesus had helped him at a difficult time. Maybe because that was a pretty brave thing to do, some twelve and thirteen year olds who were hanging around said they wanted to follow Jesus, and since then some have been coming to Popcorn.

Popcorn's combine harvester is still quite new, but it's working all right. In the future, Steve hopes that other churches will join in so they can reach more and more children.

To find out ways of getting involved, contact: Partners of Popcorn, 272 Rangefield Road, Downham, Bromley, Kent BR1 4QY.

Linda – in a dangerous country

Turn-around

Linda had always wanted to be a nurse and she loved her work. Then, one day, a six-year-old girl on her ward asked a question which worried and worried at her.

'Nurse, what will happen when I die?'

'You'll go to heaven and be with Jesus, love!' Linda forced a smile. She had to say something to comfort this child, who suffered from leukaemia (blood cancer) and had only a few days to live. Linda only wished she could believe the words herself. She had never known anyone who was dying before.

What was life all about, anyway, Linda wondered? It was no use asking her dad – a senior officer in the army. Both her parents were more used to ordering her about than discussing things with her. Linda was convinced they thought she was stupid anyway. Her twin sister had passed the eleven plus exam and gone to a top grammar school, whereas Linda had failed. Well, if people didn't notice her for good things, they were going to notice her for something! She started taking drugs and sleeping around.

It seemed so cruel when the little girl in hospital died. Linda looked for answers in different religions – Islam, Buddhism, Christianity – but nothing made any sense to her. She got drunk most nights, trying to escape from the pain she felt inside herself, but the only result was that she woke most mornings with a terrible headache.

Linda decided to make a new start, right away from home and applied to learn how to be a midwife, helping mothers who are having babies. However, she had only just arrived in Swansea when she found herself in big trouble.

'Is that your motorbike in the foyer?' The woman in charge of the nurses' home looked furious. 'We've only just had this carpet put in and now that ... that thing is leaking oil all over it!'

Motorbike-crazy Linda had not known where to leave her machine. What a dreadful start, she thought!

A week or so later she discovered that Welsh pubs did not open on Sundays. 'What on earth are we going to do with ourselves?' Linda asked another new girl.

The nursing superintendent happened to be walking past. 'Ah, you two,' she said, handing them each a piece of paper. 'Why don't you come to the nurses' Christian Fellowship, tonight? This will tell you all about it.'

'Oh no!' said Linda, afterwards. 'If I don't go I'll be in her bad books too.'

'Not a clever move, when she's head of our course,' replied Linda's friend. 'Let's both go – it'll be a laugh!'

At the Fellowship meeting Linda could hardly believe it when Nurse Val started talking about what Jesus meant to her. Linda had been working

73

with Val on the wards that week and really liked her. She always looked so elegant and well-dressed and she had a terrific sense of humour. Linda had always thought of Christians as boring.

'God loved the world so much that he gave his only son – so that we can have everlasting life!' Val was saying.

Everlasting life, Linda thought? Could it be that the answers to her questions lay in Jesus after all?

Back in her room she found an old Bible, which her grandparents had given her. She only kept it to remind herself of them. Now, though, she locked the door and started to read it for the first time, only stopping at three in the morning. The next night she did the same, and the night after. She found so many stories of people who had messed up their lives – and then God rescued them.

She knelt by the side of her bed. 'Look God,' she said, 'I've done so many dreadful things!' She listed them one by one. 'Is it possible that you could forgive someone as wicked as I am?'

Not everyone who talks to God like that sees things change so quickly and completely as they did for Linda. Suddenly she knew that she had the new, clean start she had been looking for. God was a loving father who would care for her and help her to find the right direction for her life. She no longer had to look for ways to escape or to draw attention to herself. She knew that she was loved for who she was.

The next morning, at breakfast, Linda was telling everyone what had happened. They could see a change all right, but did not know what to make of it. Normally she wore make-up centime-tres thick, but she had put none on her face that morning, nor was she smoking. No one told Linda to stop doing these things, she simply had no time for them any more.

Three weeks later a missionary called Jack came to speak at the Christian nurses' group. He talked about the country where he worked, but Linda had no idea where it was. Still, as he spoke, Linda became more and more convinced that God was asking her to work for him in that country. (Because it is still a dangerous place, especially for Christians, Linda does not want to give its name here, or even use her own real name.)

After finishing her midwifery course, she applied to train to be a missionary at a Bible College in Swansea. Her parents were horrified about this new religion and thought it was making her go mad. They even sent her to a psychiatrist, but he grew happier and happier as Linda told him her story. 'I'm a Christian too,' he chuckled.

Linda's parents would not pay for her to go to Bible College, so she had to learn to trust God for the money to pay the fees and for everything else which she needed. A College rule said that all the girls had to wear stockings (tights were not around then). Linda's old ones had more hole than stocking and she feared getting in big trouble! She prayed, and the next morning found three brand new pairs on her bed. Amazing, she thought.

Then she ran out of toothpaste, even after cutting the tube so that she could squeeze out the last scrap. Again she prayed – and found the biggest tube she had ever seen, under her pillow that night. A similar thing happened when she had to catch a train. She queued to buy a ticket even though she had no money. Then, just as it was her turn, a stranger said, 'God told me to give you this.' It was the exact price of her fare.

Later, as Linda worked in the dangerous country to which God had called her, she was grateful that he had already proved he could take care of her, both in big and in little ways. And in the end, her parents, who had been so against her religion, both became Christians.

Nurse in a camel shed!

After Bible College, Linda joined a missionary organisation and started work in Nepal. Linda had not stopped believing that God wanted her in the more dangerous country, but their government still would not let any Christians in. Three years later she heard they were asking for help. They had only five hospitals in the whole country and they wanted doctors and nurses who would set up mobile health clinics.

An American doctor said he would organise this and asked Christian medics to join him. Linda was one of the first nurse/midwives to go and one of only two women on the team. She loved the life – sleeping in a Land Rover and holding clinics in camel sheds. Snow lay thick on the ground from October until March. Linda would walk along icy mountain trails for six hours to reach a sick patient and six hours back again. Outside the temperature was twenty degrees below freezing. Before winter arrived properly, a small plane would fly in the team's provisions. They buried Christmas puddings and a turkey in the snow – and dug them out in time for a feast on December 25th.

As they ran the clinics and, later, a small hospital, the team began to get to know the local people. A few wanted to know more about Jesus, but most were strongly against Christianity. Three out of the first five people who did become Christians were murdered by their families because of it.

At times Linda wondered why on earth God had sent her, but God would always give her a reason to hope in him. One day a woman called Jamila arrived at the clinic, wearing three dresses to protect her from the cold. Linda needed to examine patients to find out what was wrong, but shy Jamila would not undress. As fast as Linda took one dress off her, Jamila put another on. Finally, Linda became so impatient that she told Jamila to ask another department for a Vitamin B injection and then go away.

Three hours later another team member came to see Linda. She worked in the dispensary, giving out medicines. 'What a dreadful woman!' she complained. 'I couldn't give her the injection she needed – or only through two layers of clothes.'

'Was her name Jamila?' Linda asked, wearily. It had been a hard day.

'That's right. I gave her a bottle of vitamin pills, but she went and swallowed the whole lot in one go. I said that could be dangerous, because they were meant to last a month. She argued that the quicker she took them, the quicker she'd get better! Can you believe it? And now she won't go away and I don't know what to do!'

I've had enough of this Jamila, Linda thought. 'Leave her to me!' she said, in a commanding voice, marching towards the dispensary. Sticking her head out of its window she shouted at Jamila,

'Now what's the problem?'

Jamila took a deep breath. 'Tell me – why do you love me?' she asked.

Linda felt ashamed. 'Oh Jamila, I haven't shown you much love, have I?' she replied. 'If you can see any love in me at all, it must be Jesus' love shining through, despite my crossness.'

Linda had a long talk with Jamila then, and many more over the months which followed. Finally, Jamila became a Christian.

Another night, a patient was carried into the clinic on a stretcher. His brother and friends told Linda that Mohammed Aziz had been extremely ill for five days. Linda realised that, if he did not receive proper treatment very soon, he would be dead by morning. The clinic could not treat him. She had to get him to their hospital, 65 kilometres away, but no one ever drove there in the dark. Bandits lay in wait by the roadside, making it far too dangerous.

'We're going to have to risk it, though,' she decided. She asked the men to put Mohammed Aziz in the back of the Land Rover, with his brother beside him. Karim, one of the local helpers from the clinic, sat with her in the front.

'I'll take a gun!' he said.

'No you won't! Christians don't use guns!' she insisted, although Karim was a Muslim by religion.

Karim looked at her hard, then grabbed a broom handle. 'You're not taking this off me!' he grumbled, as they began to hurtle along the rough mountain track.

The Land Rover roared in a low gear as Linda eased it up a steep pass between two mountains. Ahead of them the rocky walls formed a gorge so narrow that she thought she was about to drive through a tunnel. And then, in the beam of the headlights, she could see them – bandits – a whole gang of them, with guns!

'Go faster, run them over, run them over!' Karim shouted.

'Christians do not run people over!' Linda replied.

'Then pray! Pray to your God!'

She was praying – hard!

'It'll be all right now,' said Karim, turning round to the men in the back. 'She's prayed to her God. We'll be safe now!'

He means it too, Linda thought! Strange, he's not praying to his God!

They were so near the bandits now that Linda put her foot on the brake, to avoid running them over. Why aren't they shooting, she thought? In fact, where are they? The bandits had vanished. Feeling rather shaky, she drove on.

'See! See the power of her God!' Karim was saying.

Eventually they arrived safely at the hospital, where Mohammed Aziz received the care he needed to get better.

The next day Linda drove the others back down the same road. When they reached the narrow mountain pass, some local people stopped them.

'What happened to you last night?' they wanted to know.

'Why?' she asked.

'Well, we're surprised to see you safe. Just after you passed this way a lorry drove up the road, with six men and lots of provisions. The bandits attacked and killed two of the men and then stole everything.'

'Our lives were saved by a miracle!' said Karim, in a quiet voice. 'It can only be the power of her God!' After he had told the whole story, Linda was able to explain how God cares about his people – how he loves and protects them and has plans for their lives. The people who lived in that far-away valley knew that they had seen God at work – and soon a small church of new Christians started meeting there, secretly.

Altogether Linda spent eight years in that country and has many stories about what happened there. Today she spends most of her time helping other people to be missionaries, though sometimes she still travels and has adventures of her own!

Pastor Stephen – India

New Life

'Just as well we started before dawn!' panted Sunil, as he struggled up the narrow path, carrying a film projector on his head.

'Now that the sun's up, I could do with something to drink,' agreed his friend, Yohanah, pausing to wipe the sweat from his face. On his head he carried the heaviest load of all: a machine for generating electricity which weighed twenty-five kilogrammes.

The team were used to visiting ten villages every day, sometimes carrying their equipment into the area on foot, but they had never used a path as impossibly steep as this one, up part of the Western Ghat mountains in southern India.

'It's not that far!' said their leader.

'It seems like forever when you can move only as fast as a snail!' replied Sunil, once again losing his footing on the slippery track.

By lunchtime it was still winding steeply upwards through the forest ahead of them and they had no idea how far away the top might be. 'Only five hours till dark!' worried their leader, Ajay. 'It won't be easy going back down this slope with all our stuff. Maybe we should turn round now, if we don't want to spend the night on the side of a mountain!'

Rajesh agreed, 'We've drunk all the water we brought with us. We won't survive for long in this heat without finding more!'

'Hey,' exclaimed Sunil, 'isn't that a coconut?'

Sure enough, one lay by the side of the path ahead of them. A tree root had stopped it rolling down the hill. They cut it open and shared the small amount of liquid inside.

'You know, there are 30,000 people living on this mountain,' Sunil began, slowly. 'How are they going to hear about Jesus unless we tell them? And now that we've come this far ... !'

It was around six in the evening and growing dark when the team reached the top of the 2500 metre mountain. In the half light they could see well-farmed land, stretching off into the distance. A group of people from the nearby village approached, cautiously at first. They wore lunghi – cloths wrapped around their waists and reaching down to their ankles. They seemed curious about the team's trousers and shirts as well as about the equipment they carried.

'Welcome,' the head man of the village said. 'You come from the plains below?'

'We're from Bangalore.'

'Really? We have seen hardly anyone from outside this mountain since the British left India in 1947. Then foreigners used to come hunting up here, but you are Indians like ourselves!'

'You've really seen so few outsiders in forty-seven years?' asked Ajay, astonished. 'Well, we are here now to bring you some good news and to show you a film.'

'But first you must eat,' said the head man, immediately offering apples. The team had hardly ever eaten this fruit before, as apples would not grow on the tropical lands below the mountain.

After a proper meal, the team set up the equipment under the night sky. Indians love the cinema but these villagers had never seen a film before. Everyone became very excited when the generator started up and the projector threw coloured, moving pictures onto the screen. At the same time the actors' voices boomed out through loudspeakers, accompanied by music!

In the film, Indians acted out the story of Jesus' life. The people who lived on this mountain worshipped the trees and animals around them, but the film made them very interested in a God who came to this earth and lived and died as a human being. The team promised to send a church pastor and his wife to live among them and to answer more of their questions about Jesus.

'Another thing which concerns me is our school,' the head man explained, before the team left the next morning. 'We have a school building, but, since the British went, no teacher will stay up here and teach our children.'

'We will talk to Pastor Stephen about that,' said Ajay. 'There may be something we can do.'

The team was part of Cornerstone Ministries, which Pastor Stephen set up to bring the good news about Jesus to people all over India. He and the other 250 full time workers are all Indians. That is just as well because, since 1965, the government has really cut down on the number of foreign Christian missionaries it allows to work in India.

Cornerstone teams go to ten villages every day and tell the people about Jesus. They give leaflets about him to anyone who can read. Cornerstone themselves print them in nine different Indian languages and the teams give out so many that they use almost 100 tonnes of paper a year. Since 1978, when they bought their first printing machine, they have raised money by printing things for others too. Their work is of a very high quality.

In 1995 all the teams worked in one district of Tamil Nadu State. 8000 villages there had no Christians in them at all. Some of these villages are small: others have up to 500 homes. It might seem impossible to tell all those people about Jesus, but Cornerstone started doing just that! Each team visited ten villages every day, talked to lots of the people and invited them to see the film that same evening. They would show it in the open air in a place which all ten villages could reach. Afterwards a preacher asked if anyone wanted to follow Jesus. Usually some did. They were given printed Bible lessons and, if there were enough new Christians, Cornerstone sent a pastor and his wife to live among them and to build a church. By the end of 1995 the teams had preached in every village in that district and moved on to another area. Altogether, Cornerstone has started 200 churches, some in towns but most in villages.

Over the years, as Cornerstone teams travelled, they saw one great problem. The only water in most villages came from dirty rivers, ponds or tanks. People knew it was full of germs and that they could catch terrible diseases, which killed some and made others go blind. But they had nothing else to drink! Stephen and the teams thought and prayed about how they could help. A well could reach the clean water deep underground, but to dig one they needed a huge drilling machine which could travel around the villages. They had nowhere near enough money to buy one, so they asked God for it. Amazingly, by 1993 they had raised £100,000 and bought a drilling rig. Ten men take it on a huge yellow lorry into the villages. While most of them are busy drilling the well, the rest tell the people about Jesus: how he can give them living water which will satisfy a different kind of thirst, and wash them clean from all the things they have done wrong.

Pastor Stephen also realised that most villagers never saw a doctor or nurse, even if they were ill, so now another Cornerstone team visits twenty villages a week in an old ambulance. A Christian doctor, nurse and paramedic treat around 150 people a day, while another team member talks to them about Jesus and how he can make people's lives better. In one village called Nerulokop a woman's illness had left her unable to move and she had stayed in bed for seven years. The doctor's medicine could not help her, so the team prayed and, straight afterwards, she got up and began to walk. The villagers were so amazed that they became Christians – all of them!

Now Cornerstone is building a small hospital with twenty beds, to treat people who would have no chance of getting help otherwise. And the village on top of the mountain did get its school. Their new pastor and his wife used the old buildings and began teaching the children to read, write and do sums. In all these ways, Cornerstone is showing that Jesus cares.

Pastor Stephen's story

So how did Cornerstone's work begin? Pastor Stephen came from a very religious Hindu family. They would worship at the temple first thing every morning, bringing a tray of flowers, bananas, rice and coconuts to sacrifice to the gods. They burnt cow dung and wiped the ashes all over their bodies. Once a year they went on a pilgrimage all over the south of India, making sacrifices at many famous temples. But Stephen felt unhappy and empty inside. The gods seemed so far away and, even if he did the right things, he could not really understand what they wanted of him, or what life was all about.

Just after his seventeenth birthday he ran away from home and spent three months talking to Hindu priests, hoping to find some answers. In the end he felt depressed, lonely and angry because everything seemed just as pointless as ever. He wanted to give up, and the only way he could think of was to take his own life.

Stephen attached a rope to the ceiling and put the other end round his neck. Crying like a young child, he shouted, 'God, where are you? I have spent all this time searching and longing for you, yet you stay far away, so what am I to do?' He was on the point of hanging himself when he heard a voice: 'My son, there is peace for you.'

Stephen could not understand who had spoken, for he had shut all the doors and windows and checked that no one was in the house. Puzzled, he cut the rope down and walked out onto the street, where a young man came up to him and asked, 'Why are you so sad?'

When Stephen told him what had just happened, the young man explained about Jesus. 'He is the way, the truth and the life and no one can come to Father God except through him. This Jesus, he loves you. He gave his life for you. He can give you what you are looking for.'

'We Hindus worship 330 million different gods. None of them could satisfy me. How could this one god-man called Jesus change my life?' Stephen wanted to know.

The young man smiled, 'Let me pray that Jesus will come into your heart! Then you will understand what knowing him means. You will follow him and find what he wants for your life.'

'What if nothing happens?' Stephen asked.

'You can always go back and commit suicide!'

The young man prayed and Stephen repeated the words after him. He said he was sorry for all he had done wrong and asked Jesus to come and take charge of his life. At once something like an electric shock shot through his body, filling him with joy and excitement.

Stephen's parents were not at all pleased that he had found the Christian God, though. His dad shouted, 'You are no longer my son and I am no longer your father. Never come home again!'

Stephen felt devastated about being separated from his family, but somehow the peace which Jesus brought to his heart that day never left him. Homeless, he wandered until he found a group of Christians who looked after him and taught him more about his new faith. He began to pray for the millions in India who were lost, just as he had been, because they did not know Jesus. Later he joined a Christian organisation which sent small teams around the northern states of India. Their job was to tell people about Jesus.

It was hard. Often they had no transport. They slept in a different place each night, were short of money and could live for weeks on just porridge. Worst of all, the local people did not want to know about Jesus. Often they showed their anger towards the team members by beating them up.

After seven years Stephen left this organisation, travelled to the city of Bangalore in south India and started working for Jesus on his own. It was 1971. Stephen had the idea of placing opened Bibles in glass cases at main railway stations all over India. He found Christians who lived nearby and asked them to turn over a page every day. The display cases also carried Stephen's address so that people could write for lessons about the Bible. Hundreds did so and Stephen was kept busy producing leaflets and courses on the Bible, printed in many different Indian languages. Other Indian Christians began helping him.

Stephen realised, however, that they were reaching only those Indians who could read – and who travelled by train – but eight out of every ten Indians lived in out-of-the-way villages in the country. Stephen started using films and other ways to interest them. By providing them with a good water supply or with health care, his organisation aimed to show that Jesus cares about every part of their lives. Today Cornerstone is brilliant at doing just that.

To find out more about Cornerstone Ministries, write to: Pastor A Stephen, Cornerstone Ministries, Box 5006, Bangalore 560 011, India.

David Ndaruhutse – Rwanda and Burundi

Run for your life!

'I can't!' David was crying now.

'Shhh!' His sister's voice came, low and urgent. Even though the light was fading fast, David could see her eyes, wide and terrified. 'You have to, David! Come on, we have to escape!'

Their father had often used this place to cross the river into Uganda. He had placed a long wooden pole here, to make a bridge. It was all right for Hope – she was fifteen and, unlike David, had used it to cross the river before.

David was only five years old. He looked down at the brown water and tried not to think of the crocodiles which were most likely hiding beneath the surface, with rows of sharp teeth waiting for him!

The flesh on his back, legs and arms was torn and bleeding already. Only a few hours earlier soldiers had rushed into the children's house and started attacking them with big whips and spikes. Every time he moved it hurt so much that he felt like he was being beaten all over again. He simply could not cross the pole-bridge. And yet if they turned back they would all be killed.

David froze. Too many terrible things had

happened that day. His mother and little sister, Janet, had been away on a visit when the two main tribes had started fighting each other in their tiny African country of Rwanda. They couldn't get home, so Hope was in charge when the soldiers arrived. Their father had been on a preaching tour in Uganda and was due back at any time with nine-year-old Vivian who had travelled with him.

Unfortunately, they arrived just as the soldiers were madly destroying the house and everything they found. As they lashed out at David, Hope, seven-year-old Joy and even Jennifer, who was only eleven months old, the soldiers yelled that Father must die. He had given shelter to the rebels, they said.

Father had tried to talk to them calmly. 'You can see our house is just by the road to the Game Park,' he said. 'Many travellers pass this way. Some ask for shelter. I'm a Christian. If people come to me and need help, I can't turn them away.'

But the real reason for the soldiers' anger was that Father belonged to the Tutsi tribe. They went on yelling that they had come to kill him. Father asked for half an hour to pray to his God first, and, surprisingly, the soldiers agreed, though they kept him and the children under strict guard. Father asked that God's will would be done and for special strength to cope with whatever happened. After praying for his wife and all of his children by name, he started singing some of the songs he loved, in praise of Jesus. He motioned to the children to join in. Somehow they all kept trying to sing, though they turned away as the soldiers battered him to death.

Then another man came running in and the

soldiers were called away. 'We'll be back this evening to kill the rest of you,' were their parting words.

The children could see the helicopter which had brought them, still parked nearby. 'They can't have gone far!' said Hope. 'Our only chance now is to get out of Rwanda!' The border was near and Hope was pretty sure that the soldiers wouldn't follow them across it.

David tried once more to edge forward along the pole-bridge. He knew they simply had to cross this border river. Then suddenly – splash – he slipped. The water slapped against his skin and he felt himself carried downstream by the current, faster and faster. His head went under. Brown water filled his mouth and nose. He couldn't breathe. Help, he was drowning!

When he came to, they were all resting in the middle of a thick forest. Apparently Hope, running some way down the bank after him, had seen some of his clothing caught on an overhanging branch. She thought he must be dead but, when she waded in and began to haul his body out onto the bank, he started coughing up the river water.

David could not think how Hope, Vivian and Joy managed to get him and little Jennifer back to the pole bridge and across the river, but now they all had other things to worry about. Here they were alone in the forest in the middle of the night. David could see nothing in the darkness, but he could hear wild animals all around. Suddenly a lion roared, so close that even Hope believed it must be after them. The children hardly dared whisper or move until dawn broke.

Hope looked around. 'Come on!' she said. Stiffly, they began to get up when, with a crashing of heavy feet in the undergrowth, an enormous hippo galloped straight at them. David closed his eyes in terror. He knew that hippos killed more people than any other large animal in Africa. A few moments later Hope was pointing at deep hoofprints, less than a metre away. 'He didn't miss us by much!' she said. 'I thought he was charging straight at us, but look, he's having a drink in the river now!'

'Dad did pray that God would protect us!' Joy's voice was shaky.

Hope started to slash her way through the thick forest to make a path. David followed her, with Joy, carrying little Jennifer, at the back. 'Are you sure this is the right way?' Joy called to Hope.

'No – but we've got to start somewhere!'

It was nine hours before they saw the first village. Its people knew the children's father, for he had often preached there. Shocked at the news of his death, they were kind and helpful. After giving the children some food, they explained that many Rwandans had already passed through, escaping the killing in their own country. 'The United Nations has set up camps. Better go there,' they said, pointing the way.

When David first arrived in the refugee camp he had no idea that for the next twenty-two years of his life he would live in such places. At first he and the others were simply happy to find that their mother and little sister had arrived there before them.

After a few years, when things had settled down a bit, David was able to start school, which he enjoyed, even though he had to walk as much as twelve miles there – and twelve miles back, every day. It was many years before he returned to Rwanda. By the time he did, he had become a Christian and a preacher – like his father.

One day he was sent to the town where he had been born, to tell the people the good news about how God loved them and longed to forgive them for all that they had done wrong. After he was introduced at the meeting, he noticed that one man suddenly looked frightened and tried to leave the room. David thought he half-recognised him, then suddenly turned cold. Of course, he was one of the soldiers who had killed his father, almost thirty years before. The memory of that terrible day had never left David. He still had nightmares about it. Yet, as he looked at the ex-soldier, God seemed to do something inside David.

'Instead of hating him, I suddenly knew how much God loved him,' he said, afterwards. 'And so, what could I do but love him too?' David thought of Jesus on the cross who said, 'Father, forgive them, for they don't know what they are doing.' This man had not known what he was doing either. David strode over, put his arms around him and gave him a hug. 'The past is over!' he said.

The man looked relieved, but David felt something quite unexpected. As he said those words of forgiveness, the horror of the past was suddenly over for him. He felt free and clean from all its consequences at last, wrapped in a cloud of God's love, the love which had kept and protected him all those years.

Hate or love?

David woke to the sound of heavy gunfire in the

distance. He glanced at his watch. It said 2am, 21st October, 1993.

'What's happening?' asked his wife, Ruth. It sounded as if some of the others at Sororezo Mission Centre were awake. David and Ruth found a small group of them outside, talking worriedly.

'Sounds like trouble in Bjumbura.' They were living in the tiny country of Burundi now. It lies next to Rwanda and Bjumbura is its capital.

'It would take heavy shelling and bombs to make this much noise. We're all of 10 kilometres away, right up here in the mountains!'

They could hear the thump and roar of distant gunfire coming from the capital all night. In the morning, Radio Burundi announced that soldiers had taken over the country. The President and four other key leaders had been killed. Soon afterwards they heard angry shouts and smelt burning. Houses nearby had been set on fire.

'They're coming this way!' someone yelled – and now David could see a mob of Hutus, armed with machetes, sticks and blazing torches. A few had guns.

'We're coming to kill you Tutsis,' they shouted.

Not again, thought David! Why did trouble have to keep flaring up between the two tribes? He thought with a shudder that this was just like the time when the Hutu soldiers came to kill his dad – only this time he, David, was the father. His wife and children were here. He also felt responsible for around twenty-eight others who were working in the Centre, including a nurse from England and a French Bible School teacher.

'We'd better pray,' he said, as the mob began to attack the fence around their home with sticks.

'Father God, my life has been in danger many times. You know it belongs to you. I ask you now to protect all these people and to help us to go on doing the work which you have asked us to do.'

David could hear the mob shooting guns in the air now and banging their sticks against the fence – but then he saw something else. He saw an angel, standing by the compound's fence, holding up a huge sword, to protect them.

'Don't be frightened!' David told the others. 'This mob isn't in charge – God is! We're going to be safe.'

An hour and a half later, more Hutus approached the noisy mob – but David recognised these people – they lived in villages nearby. David's clinic, at the Centre here in Sororezo, had treated many of them.

'Do not harm these people!' David could hear the villagers shouting. 'So what if some are Tutsis? They are our friends, they help us!' It took a while, but the villagers persuaded the mob to go peacefully. Some of them came to talk to David.

'We'll set up a guard to protect you – but you must try to get out of here soon.' Blown-up roads made escape difficult, but David and the others decided that David's wife and small children should try to reach a safer place, along with anyone else who was not vital for running the clinic.

Three people volunteered to stay, feeling they simply could not close the place now. It would be needed more than ever! Little children were coming in with deep machete wounds. Often their parents had been murdered. David thought back to the terrible events of his own childhood and knew that he could not turn them away.

People were doing such dreadful things to one

another that some had literally gone mad – but in the past, many who were sick in their minds had been made better at Sororezo. As news about the Centre spread, many others came and found healing and help. They even started a maternity clinic, since women up there in the mountains found it hard to get to Bujumbura hospital when it was their time to give birth.

People needed them to show the love of Jesus more than ever! People kept arriving with terrible wounds and the Centre was running out of medical supplies to help them. Nearly all the bandages had been used already. They could only pray and they saw God work many miracles as wounds were healed supernaturally. Lives were changed as people discovered the love of Jesus. Now, instead of hating the other tribe and wanting revenge, they wanted to spend their lives helping people and telling them the good news that Jesus saves.

'Such terrible things have happened in our country,' David said. 'Only Jesus can stop the killing. He is the only hope for us. You know, once people really know the love of Jesus in their lives, then those of different tribes work together and help one another. We get them to build new villages where the old ones were destroyed. It's a shame that in England you hear only the bad news about Burundi, for thousands of people there are learning to trust Jesus. When we send teams out to preach about him, new churches open, hundreds each year, right across the country.'

To find out more, write to: UK office of Africa Revival Ministries, 71 Whetsted Road, Five Oak Green, Tonbridge, Kent TN12 6RT.